HEXAGON MAGIC

HEXAGON MAGIC

Using the Versatile Six-Sided Shape to Create New Patchwork Sensations

By JANET B. ELWIN

EPM
PUBLICATIONS, INC.

McLean, Virginia

**Library of Congress
Cataloging-in-Publication Data**

Elwin, Janet B.
  Hexagon magic.
  Bibliography: p.
  1. Patchwork—Patterns. 2. Quilting—Patterns.

I. Title.
TT835.E47 1986   746.9'7'041   86-16244
ISBN 0-914440-95-0

Photography by David Caras

Drawings by Deborah Christen Steinmetz
Cover and book design by Tom Huestis
    Cover quilt: *The Little Fishes,* machine pieced and hand
    quilted by Janet B. Elwin

CONTENTS

To Bud, my husband and my best friend.
Without his love, encouragement and support my dreams
would not have become realities.

Hooked on Hexagons

Hexagon designs and I did not have instant rapport. Actually, it was quite the opposite. A student brought to class a box of "flowers," the hexagon designs that form the base of the classic *Grandmother's Flower Garden* quilt. This student's own grandmother had made the flowers, but the student needed help in putting them together and making a quilt out of them.

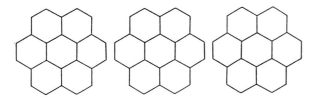

One look at all the work that had gone into those flowers and the thought of the many hours of sewing yet to come, and I wondered if it was worth it all. Not until the end of the school year was the quilt assembled and quilted. But, yes, it proved to be well worth all the effort.

Little did I know then that my future would be filled with many hexagon quilts, some simple and others complicated. My curiosity had been piqued, however, and I started my first project, a tote-size satchel with a flower garden unit appliqué on the front. Selecting the fabrics and sewing the hexagons together to create a flower was quick and fun, and many satchels were made for gifts. They were great for shopping, especially for carrying new quilt fabrics. It seemed as if those satchels would hold everything a store had to offer.

The satchel project led to some quilts. Being a "flower" expert only and not sure yet how the "garden path" was added, I decided not to tackle *Grandmother's Flower Garden* right off. When I finally did, however, I found that once I had made five "flowers," I felt like Dorothy in *The Wizard of Oz* and just followed the "path."

It wasn't hard at all, just a little confusing at first. Once I had a few pieces put together, everything fell into place.

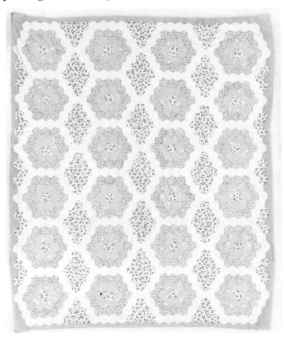

Grandmother's Flower Garden. *30" × 40". Quilt top purchased by Phyllis Plourde, date 1920, quiltmaker unknown. Hand pieced, hand quilted. Quilt being quilted by Plourde.*

That last sentence is the key to success in almost all quilt projects we undertake. Most of them are not hard, but generally we scare ourselves into thinking we can't do something new. Take the beginning steps, expect to fall a few times, but stay at it, and you'll get it done. Most of the quilts I have made have been learning experiences. It is now 13 years since I started teaching, and I have made more than 125 quilts experimenting with many different techniques. I have found that each quilt has its own unique problems, and that there is no one book that can supply all the answers. Most of the problems that arise can only be solved by working at them.

So, be assured by someone like me who has made many false starts and ripped many seams that you can and will work through the hard times of creation to complete a quilt. The secret is to make it your own quilt. Use the designs and the fabrics *you* choose, piece and appliqué in the style that makes *you* happy and quilt in the way that is comfortable to *you*. As a teacher, I tell my students, "I am here only to teach a technique or a series of methods to aid you in your work." You must feel free to use any of my methods and also to expand upon them. And remember always that we all learn by doing.

After my *Grandmother's Flower Garden* quilt, my next project was a *Baby Blocks* wall hanging. At the time I didn't think about the baby block's being a hexagon divided into three diamonds. I just knew that I liked the shading and the way the blocks fit into one another.

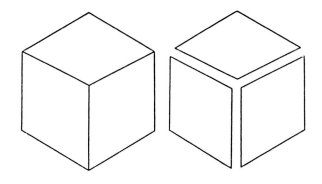

A bonus from both of these early projects was that I could use them as wall hangings and look at them often. Each time I looked at the quilts, I found my eyes roaming, looking first at the design and then settling on the fabrics in each section. There was always something new to see, a new piece of fabric or a secondary design.

The hexagon, all on its own, makes a wonderful design element. One of its most endearing qualities is the fact that it is six-sided and therefore rotates. It keeps your eye wandering. Look at this row of hexagons:

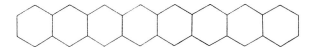

Now, when other rows or hexagons are added you have units that dip into one another rather than stacking up block by block.

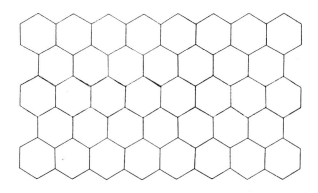

They flow into each other, melting together, so that you look up, down and all around. The more rows you add the more movement you create. That, to put it simply, is why I like hexagons.

Leaves in the River is a good example of giving movement to a shape. By redrafting a leaf design into a hexagon, the design was rotated in six ways and the movement of leaves flowing in the river became evident. This little quilt was the changing point for me. It opened the door wide to all the possibilities of the hexagon patch.

The hexagon shape is excellent for designing leaves, stars and flowers. It is a natural for snowflakes which by nature have a six-sided configuration. In fact, when I cannot think of any new ideas to work on, I always revert to snowflakes because there is no end to their design potential. Though all of the foregoing ideas come from nature's gifts to us, we can also use the hexagon shape to give new images to traditional quilt designs.

In an effort to offer many different ways to get acquainted with hexagons, I have presented a variety of designs in this book. Without getting technical about it and hoping I can avoid any monumental controversies, I have put them in categories labeled Traditional, Contemporary and Abstract. Any one design can be altered to fit into another category by changing colors and designs of fabric, so the labels are arbitrary, chosen simply to help organize and present my interpretations.

Before going any further I want to say that I am still amazed to find people who have been quilting for many years and have never tried working with hexagons. Somewhere along the way hexagons seem to have suffered from a bad press. I hadn't heard any of it until I was well addicted. Indeed, I had been sewing hexagon patches for years before I came across examples of some of the paper patchwork used in the old quilts and still commonly used in England and Europe. I couldn't believe that quilts were made by cutting out hundreds of pieces of papers, then cutting up cloth and basting the cloth to the papers, then whip stitching the patchwork together and finally taking all of those papers out of the patchwork. A lot of work. A lot of *unnecessary* work.

Paper Patchwork. *The reverse side of a* Grandmother's Flower Garden *block shows fabric sewn around paper base. Gift from Gail Binney-Winslow, S. Orleans, MA.*

I questioned a few quilters who use this technique and was told by some that papers were kept in and quilted to lend insulation. It was hard for me to imagine sleeping under a crinkly sounding quilt. Other quilters claimed that the papers helped make perfect patchwork. Though this explanation seemed to make more sense, I still found it hard to believe that people would go through all those steps when I had been making hexagon patchwork without papers and having no trouble at all. So for all of you who have steered away from hexagons because you wanted to avoid paper patchwork, please note: *No Papers Here.* I have never tried the technique and am not even going to try to tell you how it's done.

To overcome any doubts that might have been lurking in my students' minds, I used to try to sneak a few hexagon designs into my class projects without their knowing it. Recently, however, I've been coming straight out with them, as I do in this book. When I suggested starting with a hexagon sampler to my last class of beginners, they readily agreed to try. They probably would have agreed to anything, but I was thrilled to see how eager they were to start. The following week they were drafting a *Grandmother's Flower Garden*, making templates, cutting fabric and sewing. All of this with no papers. During the week, they finished the block. Each week they continued drafting designs and working their hexagon patchwork. Most of them stitched by machine. At the end of eight weeks nearly all had finished a beautiful hexagon sampler quilt of six blocks.

I believe most quilters have already seen the quilt tops with papers and heard the rumors about them. Any doubts that may have been planted in their minds are quickly dispelled once they get working together in a workshop and trying some of the techniques I have developed. Even if you have tried—and love—

paper patchwork, I hope you will want to try some of my methods. They will give you the same perfect patchwork results for half the work. I want to lead experts to experimentation, intermediates to enlightenment and all kinds of quilters—including beginners—to new design possibilities.

I have made many quilts, as I indicated, and, believe it or not, some that are not hexagon based. I always come back to the hexagon, however. After you have read this book and experimented with the directions for drafting, designing and sewing, I am sure you will feel different about the hexagon. You will discover its versatility and see how hexagon designs dance. You may realize, as I have, that hexagons keep moving because hexagons are magic.

Plourde Baby Blocks. *35" × 35". Wall hanging newly made by Phyllis Plourde using fabrics from mid- to late-1800s. Machine pieced, hand quilted.*

Drawing a Hexagon

When I started sewing patchwork, one of my greatest frustrations came from using incorrect templates. Many of these templates included ¼″ seam allowances which compounded my problems. So, in many cases I was using an incorrect design and sewing the pieces together by guesswork, really making a mess of the whole business. This led me into two new working methods: (1) using my templates without the ¼″ seam allowances included and (2) drafting my own patterns. With my new methods I knew that I was off in the right direction. Designs that I couldn't draft technically correct, I would fudge a bit. If I needed a 12″ block and the only pattern I had was a 14″ block, somehow I would rework it until it fit into the 12″ block. This was very important because many of the early fabrics I used were mill ends from the garment district. The pieces were not very big and the templates could not be any larger than the pieces. My method worked all right and over the years I learned how to draft many designs mathematically. On occasion, I still fudge it rather than pass up a design opportunity or a great piece of cloth. It is important for quilters to be able to draft their designs to accommodate their work and to save endless hours searching for a pattern in a particular size. This applies to using traditional patterns or breaking out into your own originals. I sometimes have difficulty saying "originals" when so many of mine that I have slaved over have been adaptations of old quilt patterns, furniture carvings, church windows, floor and/or wall decorations. I think you get the idea. Designs surround us and our minds are like cameras, always taking pictures. Don't you get a sense of *déjà vu* when you are working on something? Some place you may have seen that design before. We can see many of such images in our grandmothers' quilt patterns (*Bear's Paw, Flower Garden, Shoo-*

Fly), most of which they learned to draft by themselves.

Tools

When working your ideas, whether old or new, you need some equipment. Pens, pencils, rulers, paper and, for hexagons, a compass. It needn't be an expensive compass, but it must be a screw-adjustable type. The screw locks your setting into position so that the compass will not move. On occasion, I have found compasses at five-and-dime stores, but all art stores have them in a variety of sizes and prices.

For drawing very large designs, you can purchase a yardstick compass. Available in most quilt shops and art stores, the yardstick compass is a set of points, one of which is lead, that you slide onto a ruler and screw-lock into position. This is one of my favorite pieces of equipment because it allows me to make a hexagon or circle in any size.

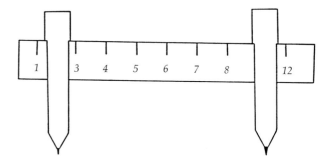

The C-Thru (brand name) engineering rulers in the 6″ and 18″ sizes are easy to work with and also available in art stores and quilt shops. You use the 6″ size when working on small-scale drawings and switch to the 18″ when you redraft to your actual size templates.

It is not necessary to use graph paper; it may even inhibit you. Most people feel they must work on the lines of the graph paper and that should not happen with hexagons because hexagons revolve. Buy plenty of plain paper, or a large roll of white shelf paper, which is what I use.

Other supplies you need are a 30-60-90° triangle, drafting tape, tracing paper and some colored pencils. Most any table on which you can put your paper makes a suitable work space. If you are fortunate to have access to a drafting table, you will have to have tape to keep your paper in place. You can also buy a drafting mat separately. You will use the drafting tape when you work with your hexagon grids (Chapter IV). Once you have drawn your grid master, you can place tracing paper over it and tape the paper into place.

When you go to pick up your compass, please don't break into a cold sweat. It is not necessary to be a geometry major to draft hexagons. After drafting a few, you will be able to do them in your sleep. My first hexagons were created by the paper folding method we used in school for making snowflakes. This I will show you in Chapter V. I feel you need a more accurate drawing when making patchwork, however; so use the compass.

Drafting a Hexagon

1. Fold 8½" x 11" paper in half, then in quarters. Center is X.
2. Open compass to 4". Place point of compass at X and draw a circle.
3. On the vertical fold, mark A at top of circle and B at bottom.
4. Place point of compass (don't change setting) at Point A and swing compass to left (4) and leave a mark on circle; then swing to right (1) and leave a mark.
5. Repeat at B, leaving a mark by swinging compass to left (3) and right (2).
6. Using a ruler and drawing straight lines, place your pencil point at A and then slide

your ruler up against the pencil and align with 1, connect all the marks starting with A to 1, 1 to 2, 2 to B, B to 3, 3 to 4 and 4 to A.
7. Erase arcs and there is your hexagon.

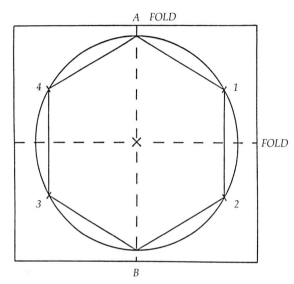

Now that wasn't so bad, was it?

I draft all my hexagons with a compass. Nine times out of ten they come out perfect. You can check the compass opening lines by putting the point of your compass at A and lining the pencil point up at 1. This line should measure the same as your compass opening. Move your compass and check 1 & 2, 2 & B, B & 3, 3 & 4 and finally 4 & A. The openings should all be the same as the opening on your compass.

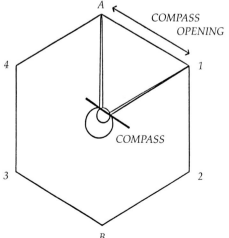

If all the openings are not the same, your hand may have slipped or the paper may have moved (did you remember to tape down your paper?). Carefully redraft the entire hexagon on a fresh piece of paper and follow all the steps. If you still have a problem area, it should be only slight. I have been told by several draftspeople that this can happen, especially working in a fairly large scale. You will discover that the larger the hexagon, the greater the margin for error. If five areas match up and one is off just a whisper, I will use the design. For more than a whisper (⅛"), I would redraft again. If you end up working with a design that has one section off slightly, make your templates from the remaining five correct sections. *Do not* work with the one that is off, because any error in your pattern will be compounded many times over when you make your quilt and this can cause no end of problems later on.

Most of the time I arbitrarily open the compass and draw a hexagon without regard to size. Generally this has not created a problem, but on occasion I have had to divide the hexagon (to make a grid) and it was much easier to work with whole numbers such as 2 into 4", and 3 into 6" rather than fractions. Also you may want to make a particular size quilt and therefore want to start with a certain size hexagon. Here is a chart of various compass openings and the finished hexagon sizes. The length of the hexagon is from point A to point B and the width is from side to side:

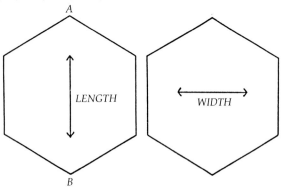

HEXAGON SIZE CHART

Compass Opening and Triangle Line Length	Length of Hexagon	Width of Hexagon
½"	1"	⅞"
1"	2"	1¹¹⁄₁₆"
1½"	3"	2⅝"
2"	4"	3½"
2½"	5"	4⅜"
3"	6"	5¼"
3½"	7"	6⅛"
4"	8"	7"
4½"	9"	7¾"
5"	10"	8¹¹⁄₁₆"
5½"	11"	9½"
6"	12"	10⅜"
6½"	13"	11¼"
7"	14"	12⅛"
7½"	15"	13"
8"	16"	13⅞"
8½"	17"	14¾"
9"	18"	15⅝"
9½"	19"	16⁷⁄₁₆"
10"	20"	17¼"
10½"	21"	18¹⁄₁₆"
11"	22"	19¹⁄₁₆"
11½"	23"	19¹³⁄₁₆"
12"	24"	20¾"
12½"	25"	21½"
13"	26"	22½"
13½"	27"	23⅞"
14"	28"	24¼"
14½"	29"	25⅛"
15"	30"	25¹⁵⁄₁₆"
15½"	31"	26¹³⁄₁₆"
16"	32"	27¹³⁄₁₆"

I find that a ½" compass opening makes the smallest unit that is easy to manage. The largest size I have used was a 16" compass opening and when that was broken down with another design within it (the *Little Fishes* quilt), the pieces were still large enough to work with ease. These dimensions will be helpful when you calculate quilt sizes and figure fabric requirements.

The most important consideration at this point is what type of design you want to work with. Before I settle in with a wall hanging or quilt plan, I will try a variety of designs on paper. I spent months poring over books and magazines before I picked out my first quilt (the *Double Wedding Ring*). It is very important that the design you finally select, especially for a full size quilt, will be one you are happy working with and looking at. No matter what your schedule is, making a quilt takes a lot of patience, time and energy. So why not make it a design you love with fabric you can't live without? Beginning quilters like to get right to it (and I don't blame them), but a little preliminary planning can save a lot of frustration in the long run.

First draw up a few hexagons in several different sizes. You may be making a mosaic or some rendition of *Grandmother's Flower Garden*, but you still need a template in a size you feel comfortable working with. If you decide to use a hexagon with a design within it, you should still draw up a few hexagons in sizes that will give you manageable working pieces. There is no need to go off the deep end with pieces that are so small they will drive you crazy. Also remember, this is not a contest to see how many teeny, tiny pieces you can fit into a

hexagon to outshine Aunt Suzy's quilt with its 11,000 pieces. The woman has nothing better to do with her time, naturally. She is better known in the trade as an overachiever. This is just good-natured kidding designed to encourage you rather than discourage you. Later there will be plenty of time to make those beautiful quilts with thousands of pieces. Right now, it's important to get going.

You may be new to quilting, or new to drafting. In either case you are experimenting and learning. Don't go overboard, but do choose something that you have not tried before and learn from experience. This is what makes the project challenging and fun.

During your practicing and experimenting with different designs, please draft your hexagons accurately. It is good practice. The more pattern drafting you do, the more familiar you become with the equipment, and it will become second nature after awhile. In all probability, you will create some of your own designs.

Piecing Hexagons

As in any pieced design, once you know the "secret"—the sewing sequence—you have relieved most of your anxiety about putting the quilt together. Each and every design will have its own assembly sequence which can be worked out by dissecting the design.

But before sewing, there is a certain amount of preparation that must be done:

Fabric

We all like to collect fabrics and whether they are old or new, the first thing I do when I come home with my goodies is throw them into the washing machine and then the drier. I do this before I take them into the workroom so they don't get mixed up with all my other prewashed materials. I cannot stress strongly enough the need to take these simple steps. There is still fabric out there that bleeds and shrinks. Washing also removes a lot of sizing, not to mention the odor that many new fabrics have. I make my quilts to be used and slept under, not to be handled with kid gloves. With all the materials available for use today—cotton, blends, silks, tapestries, corduroy, gabardine, wool metallics—you want to choose those you can take care of. Wool and most special fabrics such as silk and satin can be washed in cold water on the gentle cycle and air dried outdoors on a rack or line. There are some nice wool blends that can be machine washed and put in the dryer. Check with your fabric shop.

Ironing

Most of the fabrics I use can be taken right from the drier and folded. Some of it, unfortunately, is just as wrinkled as old-fashioned muslin. Use a dry hot iron on it and fold the fabric with right sides together and selvage edges lined up. If you iron your fabric open, it will stretch. I like a dry hot iron especially on cottons because a steam iron will leave some moisture in the fabric and it takes longer to dry. Also, a dry hot iron gives a sharp crisp finish. If it is very wrinkled, use a steam iron; then go over with a dry hot iron.

Template Material

There are a lot of different products on the market to use for templates. Ask your fabric shop or teacher to suggest some. I still use good old cardboard because I have a lot of it. After I draft my hexagon on paper, I transfer it by carbon paper onto the cardboard. Place the cardboard on your worktable, then a piece of carbon paper, and tape your original drawing on top. With a C-Thru ruler and sharp pencil, trace exactly on your drawn lines. Before you untape the original, lift the drawing in one corner and make sure you have traced all your lines. I like to keep an original drawing (especially one that has a lot of pieces) just to have a diagram to follow when piecing my material. Several times I have cut up my original and have spent more time than I wanted trying to figure out how it went back together.

To cut the cardboard, use a sharp pair of paper cutting scissors or an Exacto knife. When working on a big project, make three or four copies of each template and along the edges and sharp points put a coat of clear nail polish. This takes a few minutes to dry, but will give nice sharp points and edges that last longer. If you find your fabrics slippery (this happens with some of the blends and silks), gluestick a small piece of fine sandpaper to the back of your cardboard. Sometimes to get friction I just place my material on top of a sheet of sandpaper.

Grainline

The grainline for the hexagon runs vertically from point A to point B. Crossgrain runs vertically from side to side, and the bias runs diagonally. Grain on fabric runs vertically with the length, crossgrain runs from selvage to selvage and bias diagonally from corner to corner. Mark your drawings with grainlines and don't forget to mark the templates.

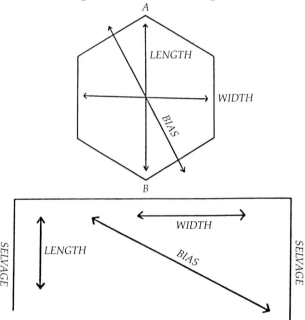

In planning my quilt layout, I almost always use the point of the hexagon for the top. This is not a hard and fast rule though. *The Good Earth* has the points running horizontally. It all depends on your final design and layout. When working with quilts, please don't get too hung up on "rules." Developing good working habits is one thing, but the minute you use words like *never* and *you can't* someone will prove you wrong. If you have a problem, try to figure out how to solve it. If you tried something and it didn't work, try something else. If you want to do something badly enough, you will find a way. By nature quilters are quite inventive.

Marking and Cutting

On dark fabrics a Paper-Mate fine ball point pen in either blue or black flows smoothly and shows up well. On lighter fabrics, I use a number 2 pencil. The pencil is more difficult to work with, but on lighter materials it is absolutely necessary. Bleeding has never been a problem with the ball point pen. When the quilt is finished, it is tossed into the washer and the ink washes out. Any ironing that is done while the quilt is in progress must be with a hot, dry iron to avoid water marks. Open the fabric and on the reverse side, trace around your template. Check your grainline. Remember the template does not have any seam allowance so leave ½" between your tracings for seam allowances. It is not necessary to draw an additional ¼" seam allowance line. After tracing four or five hexagons in a row, you will be able to judge the correct amount of space. Trace each hexagon individually so that each will have its own sewing lines.

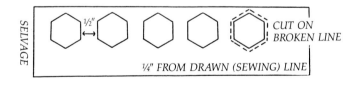

Cut the hexagons by eye-balling (guessing) approximately ¼" seam allowance. Don't get ambitious and cut any larger, ¼" is plenty. The seam allowance does not have to be perfectly straight, but it should stay close to ¼".

Sewing by Machine and Hand

Coming into quilting, I brought years of experience as a seamstress, specializing in tailoring for men and women. I also had made custom draperies and bedspreads. Now we all know that such experience is not necessary for making quilts, but what had happened to me was that I had become best friends with my sewing machine. Serious sewing with me started in junior high school and after I married and had children, I made clothing for the whole family plus my customers. It is safe to say I spent many hours with the sewing machine and that it was true love, something that started long ago when I was born. I always suspected my mother had twins when she had me. The other one was called Singer. As a twin, a day for me without my machine is like a day without sunshine.

Starting patchwork, I naturally went to my machine to put the patches together. In the beginning, the templates had the seam allowance included and that proved to be a disaster for me. It all seemed to be guesswork and that could very easily have been the end of my quilting career. I remember spending two eight-hour days trying to put together a 14" *Lemoyne Star*. The center never did meet and it was ripped out so many times the fabric started to shred. A good learning experience. All of this happened while I was teaching my first quilting class, so I had to continue. Using templates without the seam allowance included was the answer for me. The pattern line became a sewing line to use as a guide. This has been a failproof "perfect patchwork" technique I have been using and teaching ever since.

Several years after I had been happily machine piecing my patchwork, I met a group of quilters who considered it was sacrilegious to use the sewing machine. "Only by hand," they said. They really had me intimidated for a day or two until I decided to ignore them. Gram had never said anything to me about piecing by hand and, after all, she was my teacher. I continue to piece by machine and my friends still piece by hand. We are both happy in our work and that is just the point. Both methods are fine and whatever works for you and gives

you satisfaction—do it. My students are shown both techniques. Some have never seen a sewing machine and some would quit if they were told to sew by hand. Whatever method you choose, do the best job you can. With each and every piece your results will get better and you will feel more confident.

Many people who use the sewing machine are frustrated by the opening in the needle plate. Most new sewing machines are made to switch from straight sewing to zigzag, and the plate the needle passes through has a large opening. Because the seam allowance on patchwork is only ¼" it can get chewed up. Try changing plates. Use the throat plate which comes with most machines and has a smaller hole, and also change to your presser foot which has a very narrow opening. These changes may not preclude all difficulties but they will get you headed in the right direction.

Sewing by Hand

Use a single thread, not quilting thread but a good brand of polyester or cotton (if you can find it), small needle and a thimble. Start by taking a stitch in the same place three times or make a small knot at the end of the thread. Take small running stitches on the sewing line. Keep turning to the reverse side of the second piece of fabric to check if you are sewing on the line. End sewing by taking a stitch in the same place three times.

Sewing by Machine

Put needle through fabric at pin. Remove pin and take a couple of stitches, back stitch. Stitch slowly along sewing line. Every four or five stitches check the reverse side to make sure you are sewing on the sewing line. Do this by holding your fingernail along sewing line while you lift fabrics and check sewing line on bottom. If they do not line up, adjust. Do not sew over pins as this will cause a slight movement in the cloth. Keep checking both lines as you work. End sewing by backstitching to secure. In both hand and machine sewing, you must remove and replace stitching wherever the sewing lines do not meet; even a slight error will throw your work out of line. One other point: when you line up your fabrics to pin, it is not necessary to have the edges match. Because you have eye-balled the ¼" cutting line, it is likely that the edges will match, but don't worry if they don't. Just line up the sewing lines and keep them together.

Assembly of *Grandmother's Flower Garden*

(Use a compass opening of 1¼" for the hexagon)

Sewing Sequence

1. Arrange six hexagons around the center hexagon as in diagram. Pin one outer hexagon to center hexagon with right sides of fabric together, lining up the sewing lines, and pinning at each end. Now sew the seam along the drawn line only from pin to pin. (The drawings do not show seam allowances because it would be too confusing.) Each hexagon line is pinned and sewn individually.

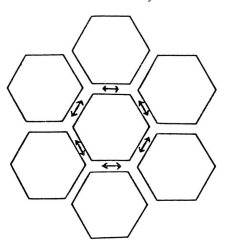

Do not try to sew around corners.

2. After all the hexagons are attached to the center hexagon, go back and sew the side seams, only on the drawn lines. Work from the inside out following the arrows on the diagram. Finger press seam allowance to one side.

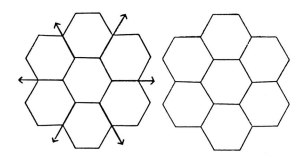

3. Now you have completed one flower garden. Let's go a step farther and put a path around so you can see how it all fits together. There are 12 hexagons for the path, which I have separated into #1 and #2. Sew #1 as indicated (step A). Then fit in #2, pin on two sides and sew on lines (step B).

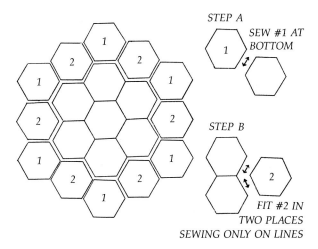

STEP A — SEW #1 AT BOTTOM

STEP B — FIT #2 IN TWO PLACES SEWING ONLY ON LINES

4. When pieces #1 and #2 are all sewn on, then sew together the remaining open sides (as in step 3). Now you have completed one flower garden with path and it should look like this:

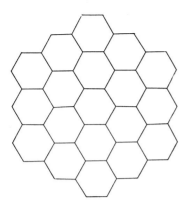

Remember to pin and sew each section separately. *Do not sew beyond pencil lines* because you need the opening in the seam allowance to fit in the next hexagon. Each time a sewing line is completed, check your work. If the front and back sewing lines do not match, *rip out and redo*. Sewing by this technique will give you perfect patchwork and make your quilt fit together beautifully. Press seams to one side with a hot dry iron, away from center hexagon. Turn to front and press.

Having finished one flower and path, you'll find it easy to keep on going and make a quilt or wall hanging. There could be no end to making flowers in all kinds of fabrics and colors, and what better use for all the materials you have been collecting and hoarding the past few years? This quilt could be a sampler of your fabric collection. For new quilters, it can become an ongoing project as you build your fabric supply.

Some quilters keep their first block as a sample. They use it as a tester block to make sure the pattern is correct and that the fabrics work together. People who feel a need to put their pieces to some constructive use may enjoy appliquéing single flowers to clothing or making satchels as I did. Here are my directions:

Flower Garden Satchel
(Use a compass opening of 1¼″ for each hexagon)

Fabric: ¾ yd. blue and ¼ yd. green cotton gabardine (or colors of your choice in any sturdy fabric). 3½ yds. readymade blue belting (1½″ wide). Seam allowance is included in these measurements.

From blue fabric cut two rectangles (front and back) 17½″ high x 18½″ wide and 15 pieces 2½″ x 5½″. In green fabric cut 16 pieces 2″ x 5½″.

Stitch blue and green rectangles together, alternating colors and using ¼″ seam allowance, to make a strip 5½″ x 53½″. This strip becomes the sides and bottom of satchel. Now zigzag all raw edges.

Whether hand or machine sewing, iron under seam allowance of one finished flower garden with path (3 rows). Center in middle of front blue rectangle about 2¼″ from bottom and 3¾″ in on either side. 1″ hem is allowed along top edge. Pin flower in place. Either edge stitch, zigzag or hand appliqué around edge.

Cut belting in half. Place raw edges of belting at bottom edge of satchel and loop at top. Pin belting on outside of satchel front measuring in 2″ from sides. Start stitching belting from bottom, stitching close to belting edge. Stop stitching 3″ from top and back stitch to secure. Stitch other edge of belting, stopping 3″ from top and back stitch. Stitch the other side of belting in the same manner. Repeat belting instructions for back of satchel.

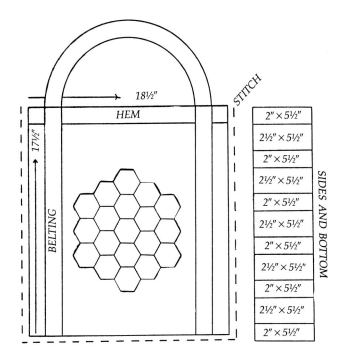

18½"

HEM

STITCH

17½"

BELTING

SIDES AND BOTTOM

2" × 5½"
2½" × 5½"
2" × 5½"
2½" × 5½"
2" × 5½"
2½" × 5½"
2" × 5½"
2½" × 5½"
2" × 5½"
2½" × 5½"
2" × 5½"

With right sides together, pin side strip to front of satchel along side, bottom and other side. Stitch. Pin back to sides and bottom and stitch. Reinforce all stitching using zigzag.

Turn under raw edges of top ¼" and press. Turn under 1", pin and top stitch hem, on inside, all around edge of satchel. Now stitch remaining belting at top.

Piecing Hexagons with an Interior Design

It gets confusing trying to decide which way the grain goes when you have a design inside the hexagon. If you drew a straight line through the entire hexagon and made a separate template with a different grainline for each, your block would be perfectly on grain, but you yourself might not be. What I do is pick one section only that will be on grain (see diagram below). This makes the piecing a little fussier because many of the seams will be on

the bias and the hexagon as a whole will be off grain. I do try to have the outside edges on grain all around so that when I stitch the completed hexagons together it is not as fussy. This technique goes against every rule I've learned in patchwork, but I don't think I could survive any other way. Carefully pin and sew the patches together with as little stress as possible and you will be okay.

If I pin a finished patched piece to the wall for a few days or weeks to study it or think about it, it sometimes stretches. The way to avoid that is to pin the unquilted top to a sheet (pin fairly close), and then pin the sheet to the wall.

When working on patchwork within a hexagon, I sew on the pencil line, but if I can stitch to the cutting line of the fabric without creating a construction problem, I will do it. This will close up any holes that may be left by only sewing on the pencil guide. Remember, this is the design inside the hexagon only. I am going to use the six-pointed star as an example to show you the grain I would choose and the sewing sequence. The arrows in the diagram below show the grainline I would use when cutting all the fabric.

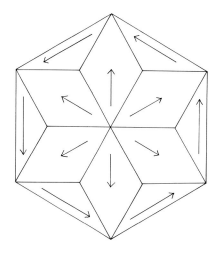

Cut six diamonds and six triangles on the straight of the grain. Arrange the six diamonds and six triangles to form a hexagon as shown in the diagram above. Set aside the six triangles and divide the six diamonds into two halves.

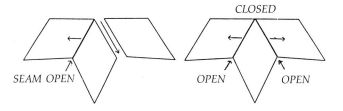

CLOSED

SEAM OPEN   OPEN   OPEN

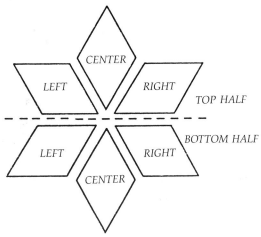

CENTER

LEFT   RIGHT

TOP HALF

BOTTOM HALF

LEFT   RIGHT

CENTER

From bottom half, pick up the center diamond and the diamond to the left. Pin the two diamonds, with the right sides of fabric together. Depending on the size of the piece, I put a pin in at each end and one in the center (this is matching up the pencil lines). Start sewing from the center. Stitch from the cutting line of the fabric, along pencil line and end stitching at the pin. This diagram shows the diamond including the seam allowance. The remaining diagrams do not.

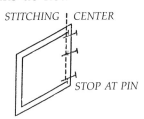

STITCHING CENTER

STOP AT PIN

Finger press seam to the left. (Arrows in the diamonds indicate direction to press seams.) Closing the seam allowance at the center will prevent holes and help the center lie flat when all the diamonds are stitched together. Leave the opening at the end to fit in the triangle.

Set bottom half to one side and make the top half in the same manner.

Pin the two halves together along the pencil lines at outside edge, center and outside edge. By finger pressing the seams in opposite directions (as indicated by the arrows), the points in the center diamonds can be lined up for easy pinning and sewing. Starting at pin, stitch along pencil line, straight through the center to the end of diamond, along the pencil line, on the opposite side. At either end the ¼"

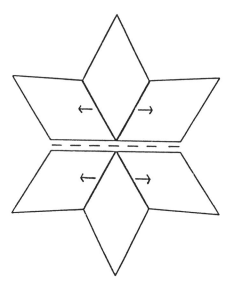

seam allowance will be unstitched. Check the front to see if all six diamond points meet. If not, look at your pencil lines to see where you went wrong.

To do the triangles, pin one side of the triangle to center diamond. Stitch from pin (center diamond) to cutting line. Pin the other side of triangle to the diamond on the left and stitch from the pin (left diamond) to cutting line. Continue all around until all triangles are sewn. The outside edges of the hexagon will have no openings.

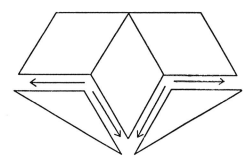

If you are assembling a quilt of six pointed stars, you stitch the hexagons on the lines only (as if you were working on a *Grandmother's Flower Garden*). Leave the seams open at each end in order to fit in your pieced stars in the rows above and the rows below.

In all the patchwork I do, I dissect the design to give me a sewing sequence and also to see how many sections can be sewn to the cutting line of the fabric. Each design is different so you will have to experiment.

Six-Pointed Antique Star Quilt. *80″ × 90″. Hand pieced and hand quilted, circa 1880, from author's collection. Close-up shows six-pointed star surrounded by triangles that form another star.*

Haley's Comet Star. *30″ × 40″, by Betsey Marshall, 1986. Hand and machine pieced, hand quilted, cotton and blends. Made in a Janet Elwin workshop, "Expanding the Six-Pointed Star Scrap Quilt."*

Traditional Designs

There is no getting away from it. When hexagon is mentioned, the first design any quilter thinks of is *Grandmother's Flower Garden*. Not only does this design have many settings, it is also known by a multitude of names:

> *Flower Garden*
> *Grandma's Garden*
> *Job's Troubles*
> *Mosaic*
> *Rosette*
> *French Bouquet*
> *Honeycomb*
> *Martha Washington's Flower Garden*
> *Rainbow Tile*
> *Spider Web*

Most of the *Flower Garden* settings I have seen have a center with either one or two rows of hexagons that make up each flower. Many of the quilts are "scrap bag," meaning that each flower is made from a different combination of fabrics and the path is made of a complementary color. The hexagons can be as tiny as ½" or as large as a couple of inches.

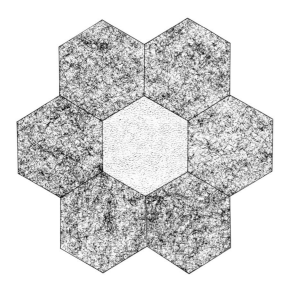

Grandmother's Flower Garden Variations

The flowers can also be separated with diamonds and triangles instead of the tried and true hexagon path.

Honeycomb

Another variation is the *Honeycomb* in which the center is a print, the first row solid, second row print, third solid, fourth print, and so on. Keep working concentrically around alternating solid and print rows.

The very name *Honeycomb* suggests a hit or miss style quilt using a variety of fabrics resulting in random spacing of light and dark areas throughout the quilt.

Honeycomb Quilt. *80"×90". Scrap quilt made by author and daughter Lea Elwin as a gift to Florence Elwin. Machine pieced and hand quilted.*

Ocean Waves

Ocean Waves is an elongated version. Start with four patches for the center and work around making every third row very dark to give the effect of waves.

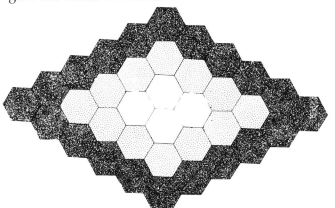

THE HEXAGON GRID

Before getting into other designs, I want to show you how to make a hexagon grid. A grid is a hexagon divided into its own triangle graph. Most hexagon designs can be worked out by using it.

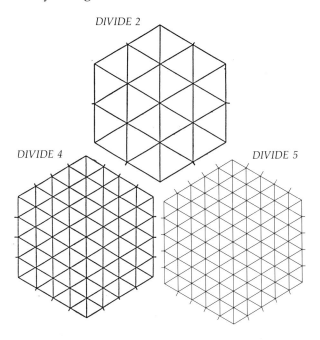

DIVIDE 2

DIVIDE 4

DIVIDE 5

1. Draw your hexagon and label the A,B, 1, 2, 3 and 4 points. Divide into six triangles.

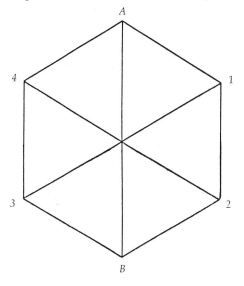

2. Measure your compass opening line (line A to 1) and divide by 2. Put a mark at the divis ion. Repeat this for all remaining compass opening lines.

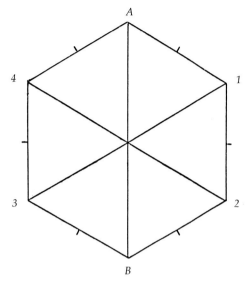

3. Now turn your hexagon so that line 3-1 lies horizontally in front of you. Draw a line connecting the marks above the 3-1 line. Then below the 3-1 line. Put a checkmark beside the 3-1 line so that you remember that you have already completed that section of your grid.

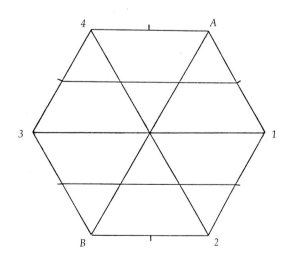

4. Turn your hexagon so that the B-A line is now horizontally in front of you. Connect the lines above and below the B-A line. Checkmark when finished.

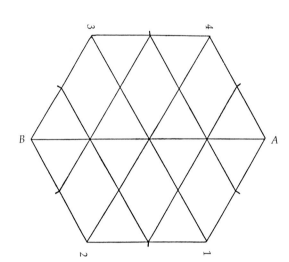

5. Now turn your hexagon to the remaining 4-2 so that it is horizontally in front of you and connect the lines above and below. This will complete your hexagon grid with a division of 2.

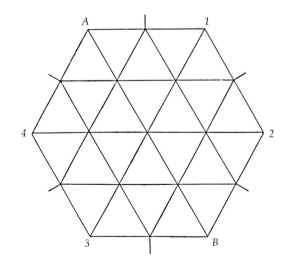

1. Baranya. *50" diameter, © 1982, cotton printed strips and crystal peu. The name Baranya comes from a district in Hungary noted for its beautiful embroidery. The quilting design was adapted from one of these embroidery designs, machine pieced and hand quilted by the author.*

3. The Boston Garden Quilt. *40" × 60", © 1982, pongee, faille and crystal peu. The Boston garden looks like this in the spring. Machine pieced and hand quilted by the author.*

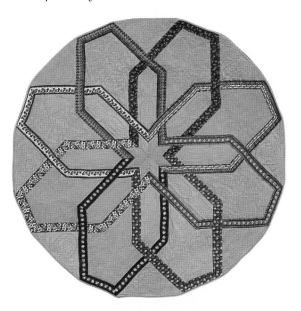

4. Ice Blue. *50" diameter, © 1984. A snowflake made of silks and blends, machine pieced and hand quilted with silk thread and embellished with silver bugle beads by the author.*

2. Ode to Grandmother. *42" × 47", © 1986, cotton and blends. A technique quilt for beginner students. Machine pieced and hand quilted by the author.*

11. A Year in the Life of My Tree. *54" × 63",
© 1986, cotton and blends. The changing seasons of the
tree outside author's work room. Machine pieced and
hand quilted by the author. Background fabrics chosen by
Sue Turbak.*

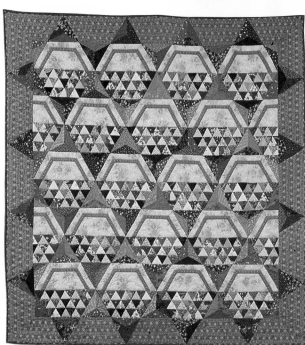

12. Lavender Blue. *58" × 61", cotton and blends.
Baskets surrounded by stars. Machine pieced and
hand quilted by the author.*

13. Paprika. *53" × 67", © 1986, cotton, drapery
and upholstery fabrics. Made to commemorate the
Hungarian jewel, Paprika. Machine pieced and
hand quilted by the author.*

14. The Good Earth.
102" × 110", © 1983, cotton, blends, mostly scrap fabrics. An off-center hexagon log cabin made as a reminder of the beautiful flower garden her mother worked in. Machine pieced and hand quilted by the author.

15. Clowning Around. *80" × 90", © 1984, cotton and blends. Author's adaptation of M. C. Escher's style of tessellated designs. Clowns have fringed hair, attached bowties and bows. Machine pieced and quilted with binding of ball fringe.*

5. Leaves in the River. *45" diameter, © 1980, cotton and blends. The use of hexagons and swirled quilting design creates a floating sensation. Machine pieced and hand quilted by the author. Leaves is a hexagonal adaptation of Nancy Halpern's* Maple Leaf *pattern.*

6. Poinsettia. *33" × 46", © 1981, cotton, blends and satin. The plaid fabric used in the bow was cut and resewn to create the red flowers and green leaves. Machine pieced and hand quilted. Background is green faille and plaid cotton, machine quilted by the author.*

7. Reflection. *40" × 50", © 1980, cotton and blends on a velvet background. From a Jeff Gutcheon Diamond Patchwork workshop. Machine pieced and hand quilted by the author.*

8. Snowflakes. *56" diameter, © 1981, all cotton. Machine pieced and hand quilted by the author. Snowflakes falling during a nighttime storm.*

To make any other grid, divided by any other number, you use these same instructions.

To help you make some quicky drawings, there is a grid page at the end of this chapter. Make at least six copies of it and tape them together along solid lines until you have a large grid measuring 22″ x 24″ (or larger if you wish). Using drafting tape, tape a piece of tracing paper over the grid. Find a hexagon (six triangles). Mark the center where the six triangles meet. If you are drawing a hexagon with a division of four, count four triangles from the center and four triangles across the bottom. This will be your outside triangle line. Repeat for remaining five triangles.

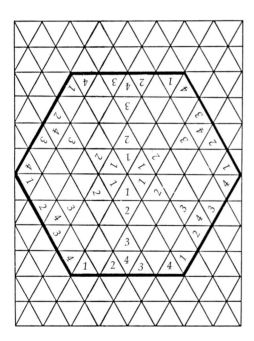

The same directions apply to making your grid with any division—say of two, five or up to 24 or more. Just count from the center and across the bottom to draw the new lines to make a hexagon grid of any size.

Use the grid to try out different patterns, and when you have decided which one to use in a quilt then you can draft it full scale. For each of the following designs, the number of divisions is given underneath the name of the design. Refer to the Hexagon Size Chart in Chapter II and select a compass opening that is easily divisible (such as five into 5″ or 10″ compass openings). Open your compass and draw a hexagon. On each of the outside triangle lines, mark the divisions, then draw the grid lines. Color in triangles, diamonds, etc. according to the drawing and you will not only have your drawing in the correct size, but also your template pieces. It may be necessary to make one or two size drawings in order to get one in which the pieces are of a size you feel comfortable working with.

Hexagon Block
Divide two

Look at the Hexagon Size Chart and select a compass opening easily divisible by two, which is 3″, 4″, 6″, 7″, etc. For this example, open your compass to 6″ and draw a hexagon. Then divide the triangle lines in half. Connect the lines, using a ruler and pencil, to make the grid lines. Color in space to create design.

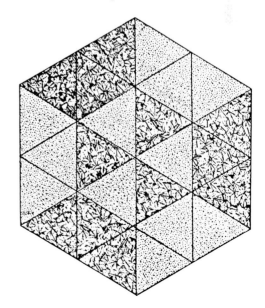

You will have two templates for this design, a triangle and a trapezoid.

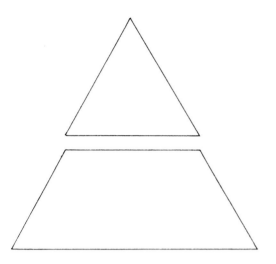

If the size of the finished hexagon is too small or too large, just redraft until you find a comfortable size to work with.

Spider Web
Divide three

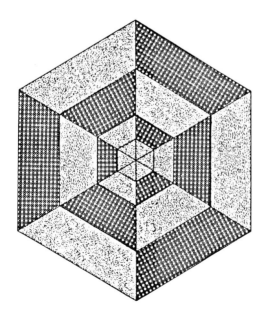

Notice the center triangles have been divided in half.

Star of Bethlehem
Divide four

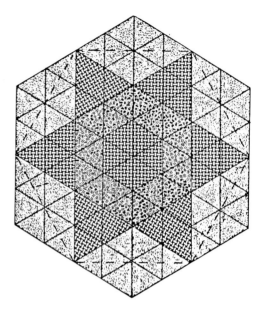

If you don't want a lot of background showing, divide diamond in half along broken line. Your new template will be a triangle, as it will be in any of the designs that use a full diamond as background.

Texas Star
Divide two

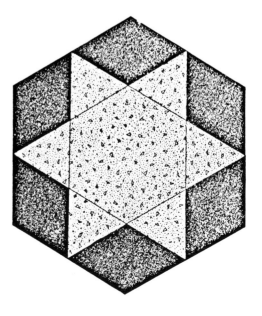

Box and Star
Divide two

Baby Blocks
Divide two

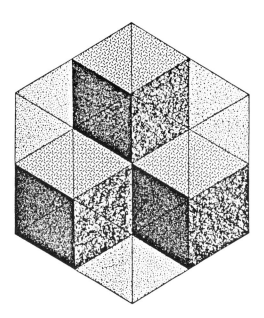

In order to get the unusual shape of the flower, you divide the center triangles in thirds. Here is the template:

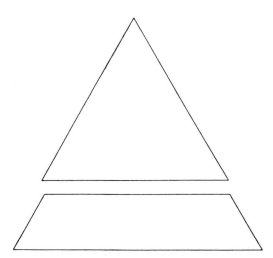

There are as many variations of this design as there are for *Grandmother's Flower Garden*. Try using graph paper to make your own arrangement. Remember the shading (light, medium and dark) is the highlight of this design.

Ozark Star
Divide four

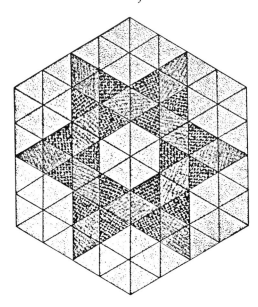

Dutch Tile, Arabian Star
Divide four

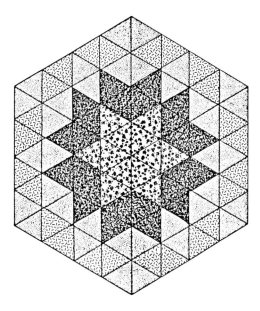

Only one diamond template is necessary for this design.

Glistening Star
Divide six

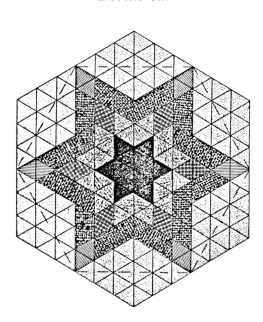

Star of Kentucky
Divide six

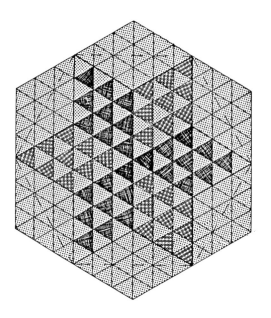

Blue Birds
Divide six

This pattern shows a lot of background to make the birds look as if they were really flying. After drafting and coloring the design, reduce the size of the hexagon along the dotted lines. This will allow plenty of background.

Mexican Star
Divide eight

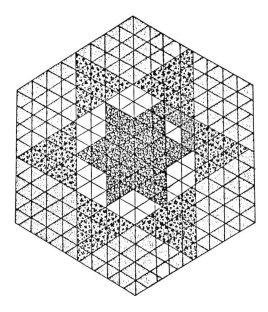

I found this design in an old newspaper scrapbook.

Seven Sisters, Evening Star
Divide five

There are two versions. If the stars are made up of two different fabrics, it is *Seven Sisters, Evening Star*, which is shown here. If all the star fabric is the same, it is called *Seven Stars* or *Boutonniere*. This design looks good if triangles separate the hexagons. The triangles will also create a secondary design of a very large star. The size of the triangle, on all three sides, will be the same measurement as the hexagon triangle line (or the compass opening measurement).

Star and Hexagon, Tiny Star
Divide six

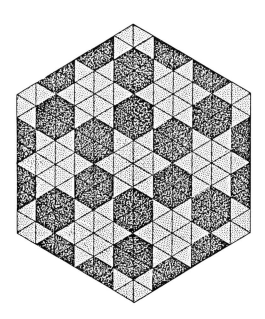

This looks similar to *Seven Sisters*, but the stars are divided by hexagons.

Pointing Star, Rolling Star
Divide three

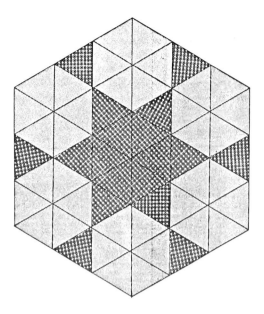

Star and Crescent, Flower Star, Twinkling Star
Divide three

Columbia Star, Star and Blocks
Divide three

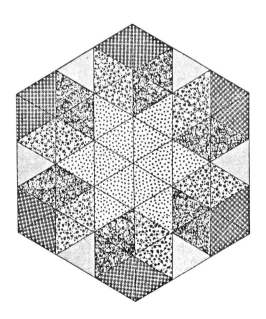

The star is pieced and the crescent shape is appliquéd. To draft the crescent, open the compass from center of hexagon to end of diamond. Draw a circle around the star. With a protractor (or dish or cup) make a curve by fitting protractor between the diamonds.

Ferris Wheel

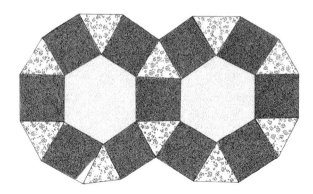

This is a "fudge it" design. You can draw your hexagon any size. The length of the triangle line will be the dimension to use when drawing the squares. Use a ruler to make perfect squares. Connect remaining lines (from square to square) to finish triangles.

There are many other traditional designs, but this gives you a good sampling. For quilt setting suggestions for these designs, see Chapter VII.

Whether you like to copy patterns exactly or make adaptations or your own originals, you can start playing with your design on the hexagon graph I have put at the end of this chapter. I suggest you make a number of photocopies because you are not apt to be happy with the very first arrangement you try. Use colored pencils or pens and make a few mockups of quilt arrangements you think you might like to work on. Use a variety of color ideas until you find a scheme you want. One of the pitfalls of using colored pencils is that they give only an impression of what you will get in fabric. It is practically impossible to match pencils to fabric, and even harder to match prints to colored pencils. Pencils, at any rate, can give you an idea, and they get you started.

Contemporary Designs

Traditional patterns can be made into contemporary quilts just by using the beautiful fabrics available today. Good examples of traditional designs that look contemporary are found in the Amish quilts. They are as vital now as they were years ago. That is because the designs are simple and uncluttered, and the fabrics are solids and bold. There seems to be no time warp with Amish quilts. The same does not seem to apply to prints; fabrics date quilts far more than the designs.

If you want to use a traditional pattern and have a wonderful collection of old fabrics, you will be making a traditional quilt. But if you make that same design from today's fabrics, you will be updating a design into a contemporary quilt. I am obviously not talking about fabrics that have been reprinted or designed to copy the old fabrics; many of these materials are used today to keep a traditional look in quilts. The fabrics I refer to are the new prints and colors that are updated with each season. It could be paisley one year and bright splashy flowers the next. Stripes or plaids. Solids in earthy tones or very pale ice cream shades. Fortunately for us, our stores are filled with lots to choose from; though it always seems that when I want to make a blue quilt, I can't find the blue fabrics I need. That's because fabric manufacturers change colors each season along with the clothing styles. Check your stores and you will get a good idea of what colors will be popular in the upcoming season. If I still want to make a blue quilt, I hang in there. Eventually, I will find just what I'm looking for.

As I said, the choice of fabric alone can give a traditional design a contemporary look. But you can also change the traditional look by adapting the patterns. Many quiltmakers are elaborating on old favorite designs and sometimes simplifying them. The six-pointed star is a good example of the simplification of a design. Most beginner quilting classes use an eight-pointed star as a technique lesson. There are many expanded eight-pointed stars which can be redrafted into six-pointed stars and variations. Now just think about this a minute. Only six points to match in the center instead of eight. That alone should be worth at least one try. Taking the design further and expanding the stars will give you beautiful radiating quilts with much less cutting and piecing. Doesn't that sound enticing?

The following are examples of six-pointed stars and variations on expansion. Two of the simplest and most easily adaptable designs are Star A and Star B. Use a hexagon grid when drawing these stars:

Star Mobile. *A six-pointed star variation, this two-sided mobile is made from metallic and cotton fabrics, machine pieced and quilted with metallic thread. Designed by author especially for the New England Quilter's Guild April 1985 meeting.*

Six-Pointed Star A
Divide two
12 diamonds of equal size

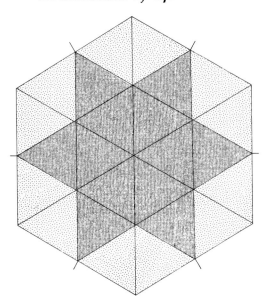

Six-Pointed Star B
Divide two
Six diamonds and six triangles

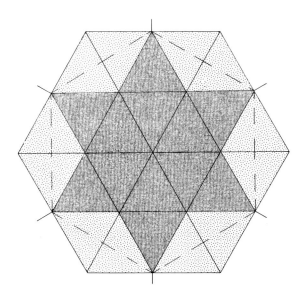

Divide the background diamond in half along the broken lines. Sometimes when you are butting the stars you will not want as much background showing. Use triangles as a background, and this will form diamonds when the stars are pieced together.

The eight-pointed star variations have names such as *Blazing Star*, *Harvest Star*, *Star of Bethlehem* or *Broken Star*. These are multiple rows of diamonds, from two rows to ten or more. By using the diamond, taken from the hexagon shape, you cut down the number of pieces to work with. Again, instead of eight diamonds to fit together in the center, you will have only six. The following are designs based on the eight-pointed star patterns. We are also changing the names to differentiate between the two:

Bright Star
Divide four
Two rows

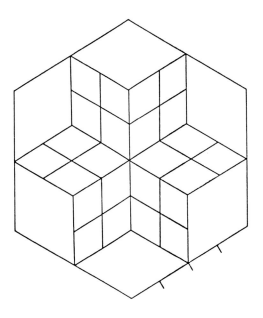

Autumn Star
Divide six
Three rows

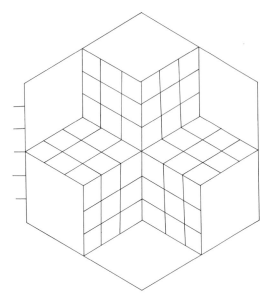

Radiant Star
Divide 24
Six rows

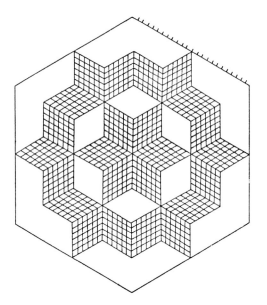

North Star
Divide 12
Six rows

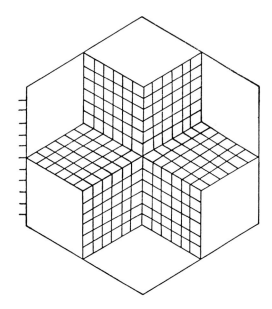

When you want to draft your own stars, look for the number of divisions to make in each hexagon. It is given with each design and is important to know if you need a particular size hexagon. You don't need it when the diamond is the only piece you use for a template. At the end of this chapter there is a whole page of diamonds in different sizes. You can also use them as triangles if you trace half a diamond—along the broken line.

When using the diamonds, you will have to do some simple math in order to determine the finished sizes of the piece you are planning.

Example:
By using the length (3½") of the diamond and multiplying it by the number of diamonds (4) in the length of the hexagon, you will arrive at the finished length of the hexagon. 3½" x 4 diamonds= 14" length. For the width, measure the side of the diamond (2"). The side and center diamond

measurement *will be the same. Multiply it by the number of diamonds (six) across the longest row. 2" x 6 diamonds=12" width.*

Bright Star
12" x 14"

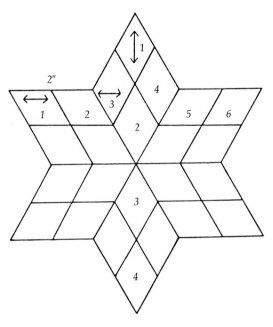

If you need a diamond of another size, use your 30-60-90° triangle to draw one as follows: Fold paper in half, then quarters.

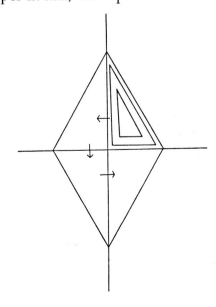

Flip triangle to reverse. Follow arrows to complete diamond. Half the diamond is a triangle.

Background Diamonds and Triangles

To figure the size of the background diamond and/or triangles, measure the side of the diamond and multiply by the number of diamonds in a row. Again, fold paper and use a 30-60-90° triangle to draw these pieces:

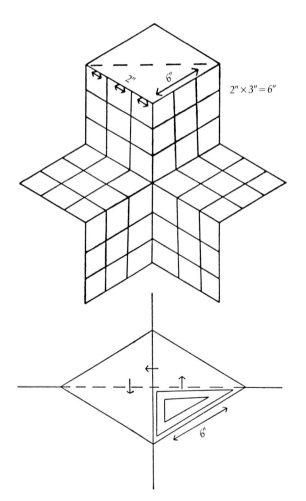

Sometimes the pieces you are drawing are longer than your triangle. Either buy a triangle a larger size or if it is a matter of only a couple of inches, extend your triangle by taping a ruler to it. Remember that the diamonds and triangles you are drawing are the finished sizes. Always cut seam allowance ¼" larger all around.

When sewing "whole cloth" (the diamonds and/or triangles) to a patchwork area (the pieced star in this case), try this notch method to help distribute fabrics evenly.

Example: If the sides of the small diamonds measure 2", with a pencil mark a notch every 2" in the seam allowance on your whole cloth diamond/triangle. Align notches with seams of pieced star, easing fabrics to fit within the notch marks. Pin. Stitch on seam line working from the center out. Remove pins. Repeat for the other half of diamond/triangle.

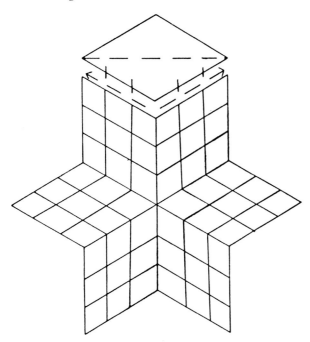

When you are stitching a straight piece of fabric such as the diamond, the triangle, lattice work or a border, it is very difficult to distribute the fabrics evenly without using this technique. Fabrics have a tendency to do their own thing especially those with a lot of give. Anything we can do to ease the frustration of stitching 24 diamonds to a single triangle edge should be tried. I have used this method for a long time, and it does help.

Use the hexagon grid at the end of Chapter IV, if you would like to have a small scale drawing for working out colors. Place tracing paper over the hexagon grid and draw the design you want to experiment with. Find the six-pointed star, then try *Bright Star*. Once your eyes get used to finding the lines, you will be able to pick out the diamond shapes you need, then the triangles, and so on. As with anything new, you need to practice. I find repeating steps and procedures time consuming, but very rewarding. You will find the key to the patterns and this will give you the power to go on to new and exciting discoveries.

The Stone Wall Quilt

One of the discoveries I have made over the years designing and making quilts has been the value of determination. I have been fortunate in meeting many superb quilt artists and hearing them talk. Most of these people have shared their successful quilt experiences, but the ones I learned the most from were those who told about their disasters. We all have them. But determination keeps us going. For myself, I know once I get an idea, no matter how discouraged or how much ripping out and redrawing and redrafting I do, I have to see the end result. There has been only one quilt I never finished. The whole idea was beyond me at the time, and I got so annoyed that I threw that quilt away and came up with another idea.

The *Stone Wall* quilt could have been one of those throw-away projects. I once had the idea that I wanted to work with brown fabrics, so I collected a good variety of materials and then tried to figure out how to use them. When I came up with the idea for a curved hexagon, I had no idea how to make it. Then I remembered folding paper snowflakes in school. After I folded my paper and came up with the correct size hexagon, I had to draw in the curved sections. This I did freehand making each arc different. That didn't phase me in the least. I very happily made my different templates, cut up my fabric and sewed the curved hexagons. Now what to do? Because the majority of the quilts I worked were lattice style, I naturally chose lattice work which then developed into the diamonds separating the hexagons (the diamonds are the mortar and the hexagons, the stones). After I had put on the first solid color border I ran into my problem with the patchwork border. Because many of the stone walls in my area have little stones and rough surfaces along the tops (to discourage children from walking on them, I assume), I chose the curved pieced border. I wasn't sure if this was right or not and ran around asking my friends their opinions. Each and everyone had a different viewpoint, and this was now making me crazy. I rolled the quilt up in a ball and threw it in the corner where it lay for almost a year. This is the only time I have ever abandoned a good idea. I knew that basically I liked the quilt and that I just needed some confidence. One day I read a book about a person and his great idea. He had told so many people about his great idea, and they offered so many suggestions and changes that his own great idea soon disappeared. In its place were everyone else's great ideas. He decided to go ahead and work on his own. I thought immediately about my quilt

rolled up in the corner. I made the decision then and there to continue with my original idea and not to change anything. I finished the quilt and it has been one of my favorites ever since. I want to share with you the design and templates of my updated version of the original *Stone Wall* quilt:

Fabric: (45" wide) ten pieces ½ yd. brown prints, 2 yds. grey, 3 yds. solid brown

Size: 97¼" x 102½"

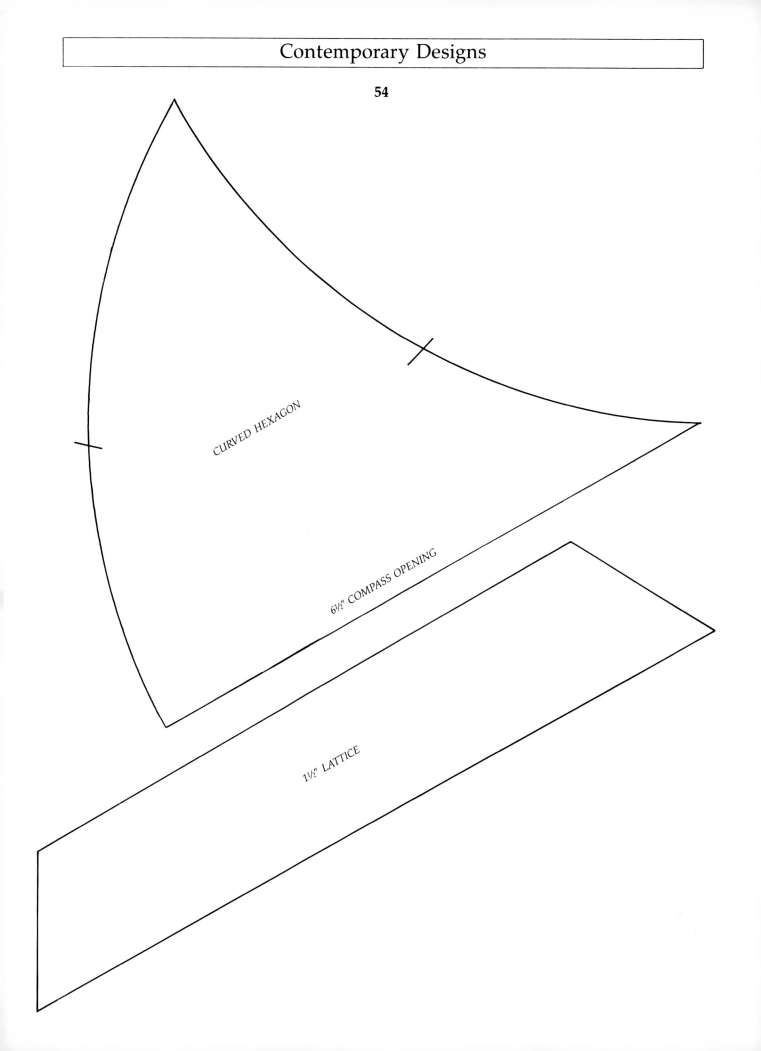

CURVED HEXAGON

6½" COMPASS OPENING

1½" LATTICE

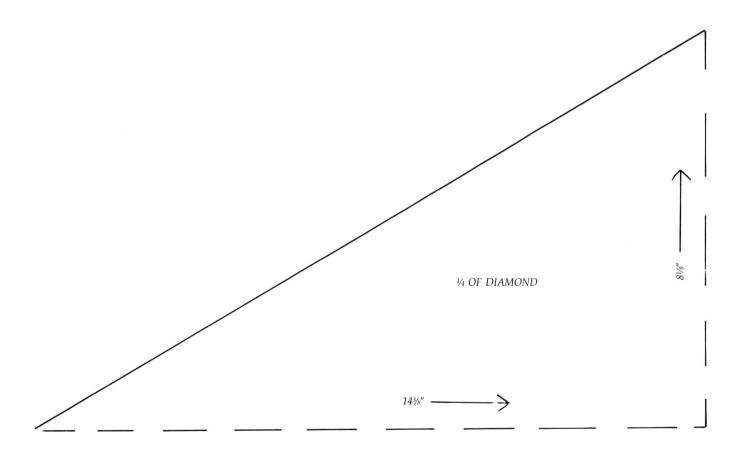

¼ OF DIAMOND

8⅛"

14⅜" ⟶

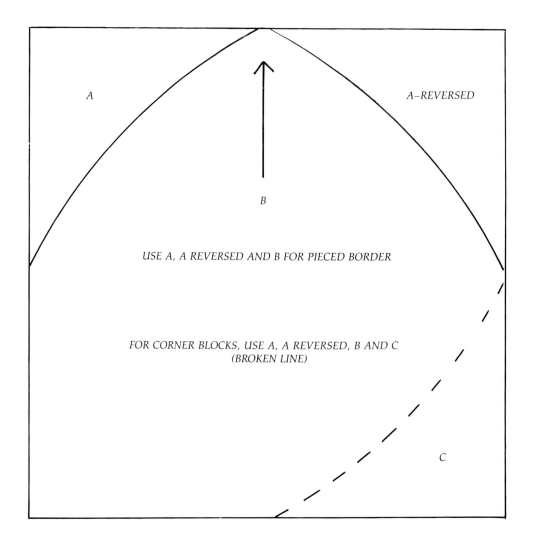

A

A–REVERSED

B

USE A, A REVERSED AND B FOR PIECED BORDER

*FOR CORNER BLOCKS, USE A, A REVERSED, B AND C
(BROKEN LINE)*

C

I have made a few changes so that the design will be easier for you to work:

1. The curves are now all the same and the template has the notch marks on it.
2. The lattice is one template. After you have assembled a complete curved hexagon, attach lattice all around and then sew a row of hexagons together. (Please notice that all these templates *do not* have the seam allowance included and you will be sewing on your marking lines.)
3. The diamond shape has been changed in the redrafting.
4. When you work on the pieced border, make four corner blocks with the curve on three sides. This gives a better flow around the border.

Most of these changes are not apparent from comparing the picture of my quilt and the new diagram. The improvement is mostly in the assembly, and I do think the border is easier on the eyes now.

The measurements for the solid fabric borders are given on the diagram. They are not mitered. I have one very important and helpful technique for attaching solid fabric, whole cloth, or lattice to a pieced border or block. It involves, again, notches.

Refer to your original diagram. *Do not* measure your finished blocks or pieced section to get your measurements, but check your diagram. If you have made a 12" block, according to your diagram, then you need 12" lattice work. As I have said before, fabric has a tendency to do its own thing, especially a pieced block; and change is compounded when you have a pieced border, so your correct measurements are those in your diagram. When you measure a pieced border, because of all the seams, it may have a tendency to grow or shrink. By cutting your lattice or whole cloth border according to your diagram, you will fit these pieces in correctly giving you nice smooth lattice strips and borders.

Cut your border including ¼" seam allowance on all sides. The first side borders would be 5⅛" x 82" plus ½" which would be 5⅝" x 82½".

After the border is cut, mark your ¼" seam allowance all around the edge. In the seam allowance mark the notches for the quarter diamonds (4¹⁄₁₆"), the finished hexagon including the lattice (8¼") and the half diamonds (8⅛"). (Refer to the diagram for *Stone Wall* to see notches on right hand, 5⅛″ x 82″ border.) Pin the notches on the border to the corresponding patchwork on the pieced quilt. In some cases you may have to ease the fabric to fit by basting. After you have pinned the border in place, stitch.

By taking these extra steps and marking notches and distributing your fabric correctly along the border, you will have a perfect fitting border.

Attach both side borders. Then mark and fit top and bottom borders in the same manner. Check diagram for dimensions. Don't forget to add seam allowance. For top and bottom borders, you will have 5⅛″ on either end of fabric (to cover side borders), then mark notches for quarter diamonds and half diamonds. Pin and stitch.

All along the raw edge of all the borders mark notches every 5⅛″ to fit in the pieced border.

Cut final border and mark seam allowance. Check diagram for dimensions and add ½″ for seam allowance. Mark notches every 5⅛″, pin to pieced border, ease and stitch. Stitch side borders first and then top and bottom.

Tumbleweeds

This wall hanging is a variation of the *Stone Wall* quilt. It uses a smaller compass opening for the curved hexagon and the blocks are set together with no lattice work so they flow into one another. By using a monochromatic color scheme the entire quilt can be made to look like a tumbleweed with its shading of light and dark spots. I discovered that if I kept my compass opening the same I could draft perfect curves.

Here is how you do it: Open compass at 5″ and draw your hexagon. Keep compass opening the same (5″) and put compass point at A with pencil point in center of hexagon. Draw

arc to 1. Next, move compass point to 1. With pencil point at center, draw arc to 2. Continue around hexagon until you have six arcs. To make the notch, close compass to 2½″. Place point in center as if you were drawing a circle, but only place a mark on the arcs. This will give you even notch marks all around.

Ocean Odyssey

When I made the *Stone Wall* quilt, I enjoyed working with this curved hexagon so much that I knew I would be making another quilt, but an ocean version. For years I collected "ocean" fabric. I started out by buying three and four yards at a time figuring that when I had about eight different fabrics I was going to start the quilt. Somehow, the timing wasn't right and the fabric kept sitting there. I kept buying more but began cutting the amount to one and two yard pieces, then down to a half and finally a quarter of a yard. All of a sudden the idea came to me that if I combined my favorite curved hexagon and a beautiful design that I have loved for years, *Ocean Waves*, I could make a great quilt.

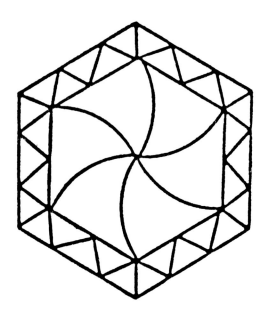

Sitting amid my great pile of fabric, I wondered how much I had actually bought. It came to 72 yards! Because of the large variety of materials I had, I didn't use much more than a quarter to a half yard of each piece. I decided that in the future, I would still buy lots of fabrics but in smaller amounts. I especially liked picking out different fabrics for each of the blocks I made so that even though the quilt had a repetitive design, each and every block was different. That made the sewing exciting.

Snowflakes

I love making snowflakes. First, because each and every one can be different and, second, because they are hexagons. There are many variations and techniques used in snowflake making. I would like to share three of my favorites with you.

Appliquéd Snowflakes

These snowflakes are made using the paper folding technique. You can use a square of any size. For this example I have used 8½" x 8½". First fold the square in half. Then in thirds.

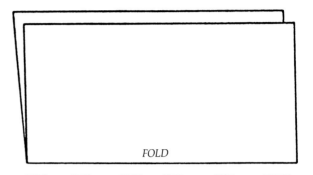

FOLD

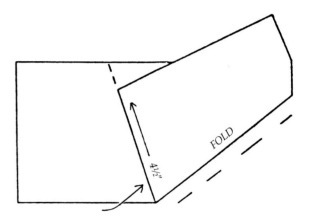

FOLD

4½"

Measure from center, along outside edge 4½"
(this measurement will change when you use a
different size paper) and mark each side. Connect marks and cut away excess. Fold again.
Place pattern sample along folded edge, draw
and cut away excess paper. Or cut, free hand,
along folded edge for your own pattern. For
this particular technique, cut pattern in area to
the left of the broken line in the diagram. After
you have made a few samples, you will understand what is happening here and you may
want to experiment.

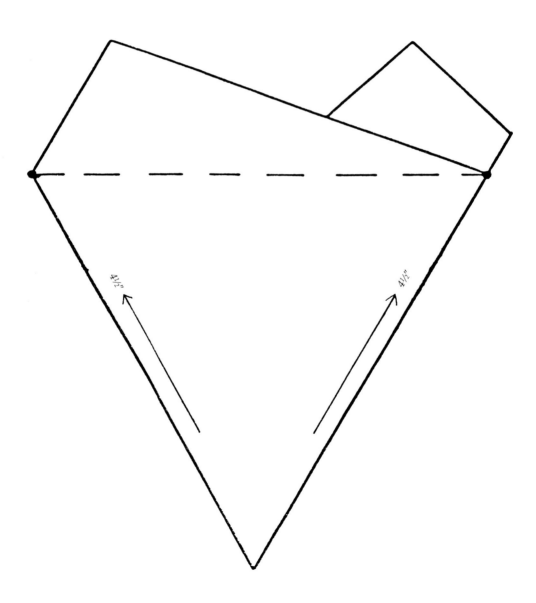

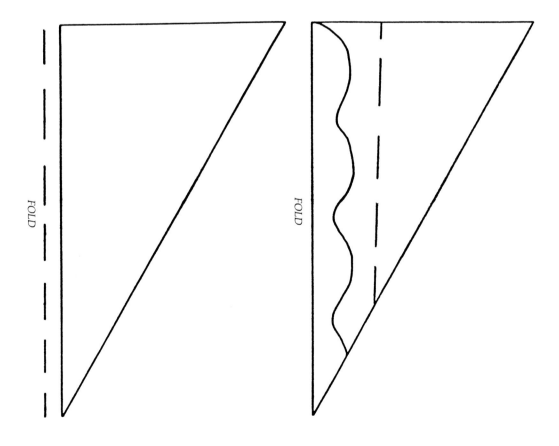

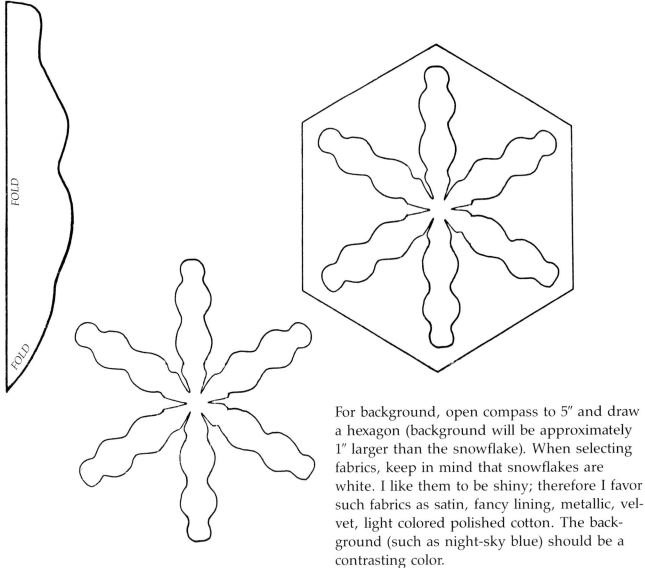

For background, open compass to 5″ and draw a hexagon (background will be approximately 1″ larger than the snowflake). When selecting fabrics, keep in mind that snowflakes are white. I like them to be shiny; therefore I favor such fabrics as satin, fancy lining, metallic, velvet, light colored polished cotton. The background (such as night-sky blue) should be a contrasting color.

It is not necessary to add seam allowances to either piece. Cut two hexagonal background pieces and one snowflake. (If the fabric is very flimsy, you may want to line it with cotton so that you can't see the background fabric through it.) Center snowflake on one background piece and hand appliqué or zigzag it in place. I generally use the zigzag because I like the outlining of the snowflake.

Cut a piece of polyester or cotton batting (for body) and baste appliquéd snowflake, batting and the other background together. Quilting is optional. Bind. (See binding in Chapter X.)

Depending on the size you make, these snowflakes can be used as tree ornaments, mobiles, window decorations or shade pulls. Use fish line (available in sporting goods stores) to make loops for hanging.

If you make them large enough, they would be pretty as a winter wall hanging or the beginning of a quilt. To make a larger size, just fold your paper in larger squares, and cut your pattern. Remember to cut your background hexagon larger.

Cutwork Snowflakes

These are my favorites, but they are also the pickiest to make. They are cutwork snowflakes with no background. I have made them in a variety of sizes, some from silver metallic for a 20-piece mobile and a few larger ones from shimmery drapery fabric that I hang individually in my kitchen in winter.

Snowflake Mobiles. *Three different snowflakes made by author from antique satin drapery fabric, 1980. Machine stitched. These hang in her kitchen during winter months.*

Use paper folding method for patterns. Measure sides 3¾". These measurements change with different size snowflakes, of course. If you want a larger pattern, fold larger square and measure sides longer, and reverse procedure for smaller hexagons. Cut away excess paper. Fold and place sample pattern along fold line, or cut your own pattern. Notice on this type snowflake, you do not cut away all of the fold on the right side of the paper. Because there is no background, the snowflake has to connect all around for support.

Example: Trace and cut pattern along lines; do not cut where snowflake pattern meets the fold. Open paper to see entire snowflake.

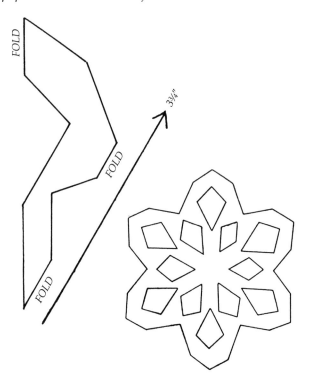

Cut two squares of snowflake fabric at least ½" larger than your snowflake pattern. Cut one batting the same size as fabric. (I like Fairfield's Cotton Classic because it gives body without bulk.) Baste the three layers together. Pin snowflake pattern on top of fabric and then

place all on top of a clean piece of white paper. The white paper will be a base to keep fabric from slipping when you are sewing.

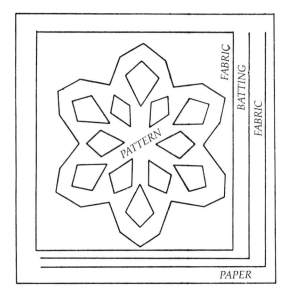

Stitch along snowflake pattern edges with straight stitch. Rip away base paper. Cut away background fabric as close to stitching line as possible. Stitch all edges using zigzag. [You may have to use another piece of base paper if your fabric is too slippery.] I stitch around pattern twice so that zigzag is very thick. Dip in

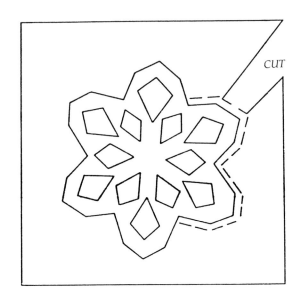

liquid starch (made from directions on bottle for a strong solution). Let dry on cookie rack. Use fishing line to make loops for hanging.

All of these snowflake patterns are just samples. Once you have made one, you can make as many different snowflakes as you want. Here is a pattern for another one:

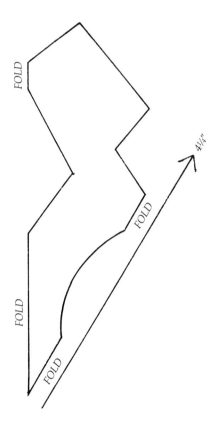

This snowflake is a little larger. Measure sides of paper 4¼", fold again and place pattern along folds. Trace and cut pattern along lines. Open paper to see entire snowflake. Follow directions for the smaller cutwork snowflake.

Pieced Snowflakes

During the holiday season, newspapers, schools and store windows are full of snowflake designs. I got the idea once to make a snowflake wall hanging using a different pattern for each block. I took a newspaper ad that had many designs on it and adapted a few of the patterns. When I looked at one, I visualized *Grandmother's Flower Garden* as a base and then incorporated my drawing within it. Here is a sample of one of these blocks in my *Snowflake Wall Hanging*. This will measure 20″ x 21″. Fabrics can be anything you want them to be. I used cotton; but any fabric could be used, especially if you are planning to make a wall hanging rather than a quilt.

As you see in this drawing, the center hexagon design flows into the outer hexagons. In designing this snowflake I didn't use any particular technique or mathematical solution. I suggest you begin by drawing a *Grandmother's Flower Garden*. Working with tracing paper, try to copy a design onto it from a newspaper or book. It helps to remember that you need a center and six spokes.

Here are the templates for my snowflake design. You will be piecing one center and six spokes. When marking the fabric for the spokes, check your templates. Most of the pieces have a reverse (marked R in illustrations). In order to remember this, mark the appropriate templates (cut six and R). When marking the fabric, place an R in the seam allowance for the reverse pieces. Piece center first. Attach spokes to the center, lining up notches.

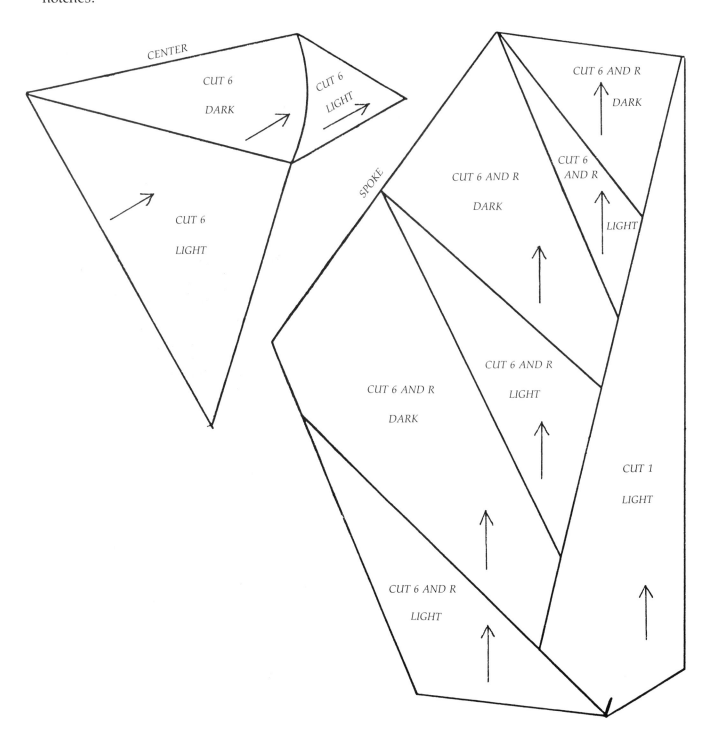

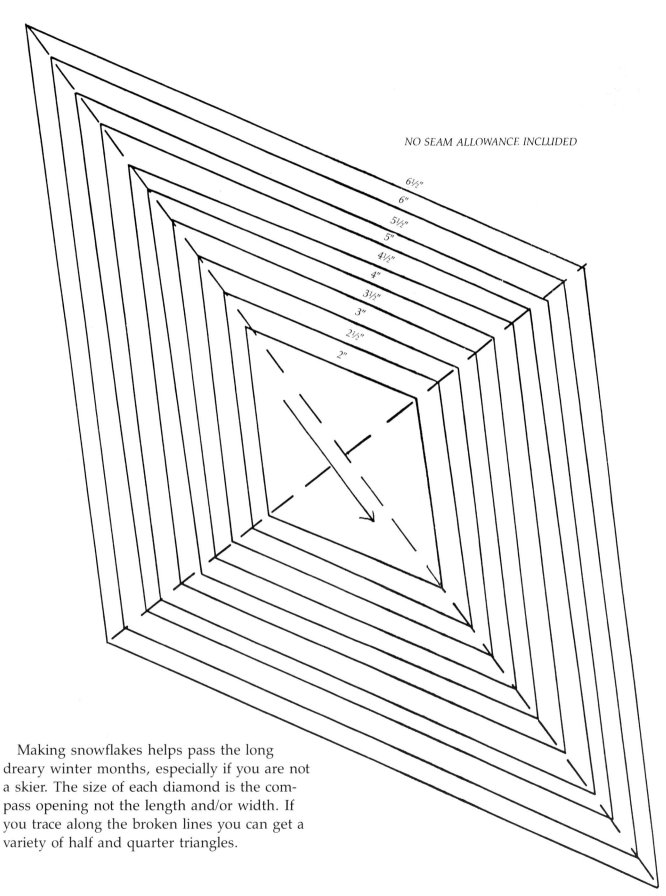

NO SEAM ALLOWANCE INCLUDED

6½"

6"

5½"

5"

4½"

4"

3½"

3"

2½"

2"

Making snowflakes helps pass the long dreary winter months, especially if you are not a skier. The size of each diamond is the compass opening not the length and/or width. If you trace along the broken lines you can get a variety of half and quarter triangles.

The sizes of the curved hexagons and hexagons are the compass openings. To make the notch marks on the curved hexagon, open compass to half (of whichever size you choose), put point in at top of design and mark notches on each side of curve (see 6½" *Stone Wall* design). Hexagons can be used whole or trace dotted lines to use as trapezoid.

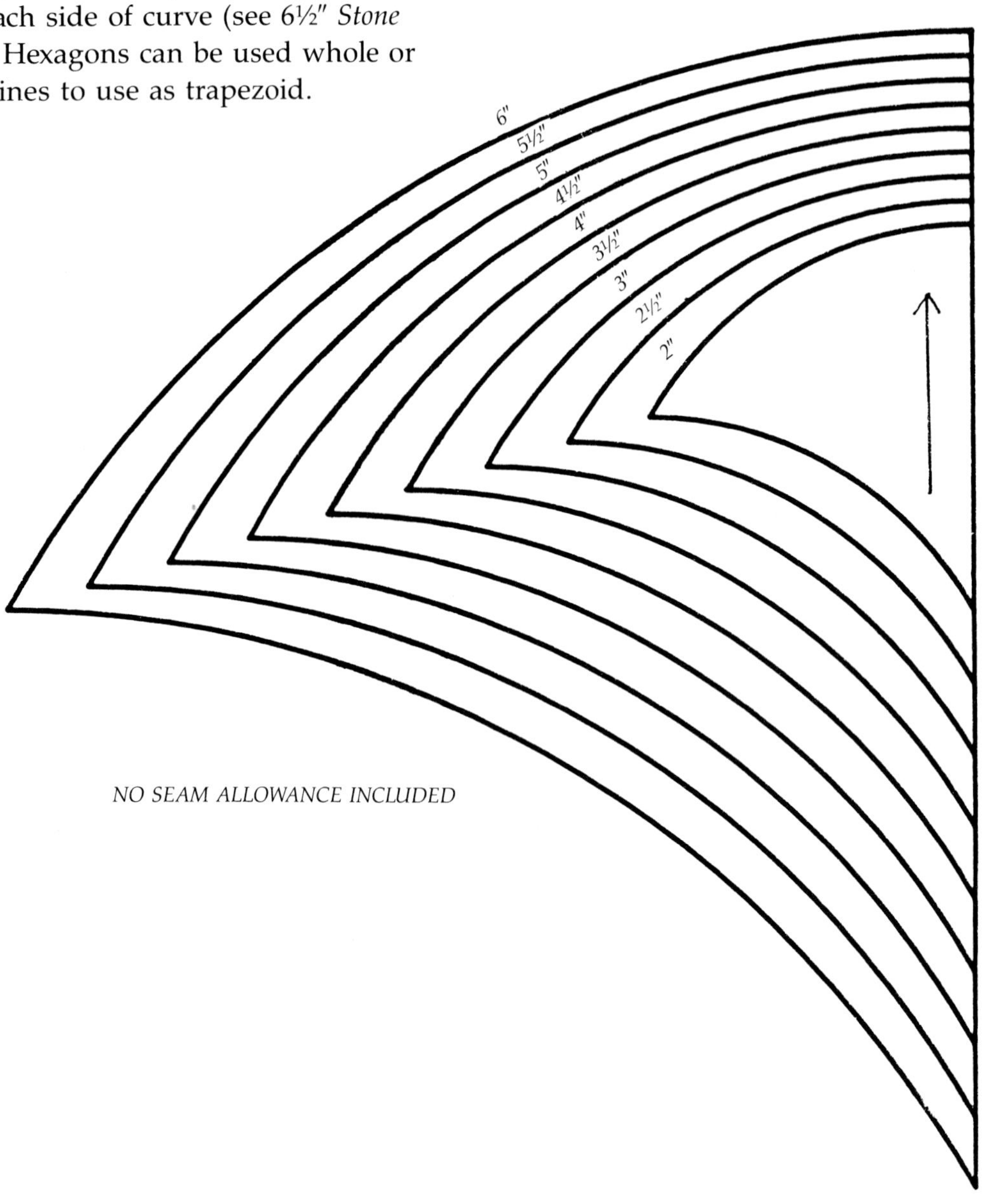

6"
5½"
5"
4½"
4"
3½"
3"
2½"
2"

NO SEAM ALLOWANCE INCLUDED

9. Silver Mobile. © 1980, silver lamé mobile with 20 different cutwork snowflakes. This hangs in author's dining room during the winter months.

10. The Crown Jewel. 80" × 90", © 1985, cotton and blends. Made by author as a 25th Anniversary gift for her husband. Machine pieced and hand quilted with silver metallic thread. The idea for this quilt came to her while watching the PBS special, "The Jewel in the Crown."

17. Ocean Odyssey. *80" × 82", © 1983, cotton blends. Machine pieced and hand quilted by author. This quilt is her reflection of the family's favorite vacation spot, an island in Maine.*

16. The Little Fishes. *80″ × 82″, from a collection of fabrics given to author by New England Images I Quilt Show Committee, a show sponsored by The New England Quilters Guild in Topsfield, MA to help establish a quilt museum in New England. Quilt was made as a surprise for Spring 1984 meeting when Mrs. Elwin was guest speaker. Machine pieced and hand quilted with* Dune Point *border.*

18. Tumbleweeds. *45″ diameter © 1981; all cotton. Machine pieced, hand quilted by author and given to her husband to make amends for getting behind in her housekeeping. At the Elwins' house, dust kitties are called tumbleweeds.*

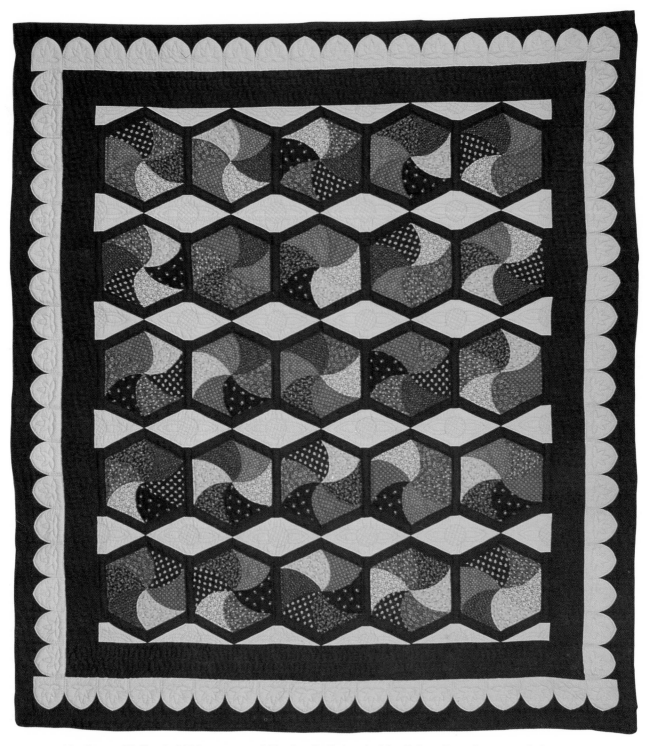

19. Stone Wall. © *1978, cotton and blends. Quilt inspired by Robert Frost lecture and the many beautiful stone walls in New England. Machine pieced and hand quilted by author.*

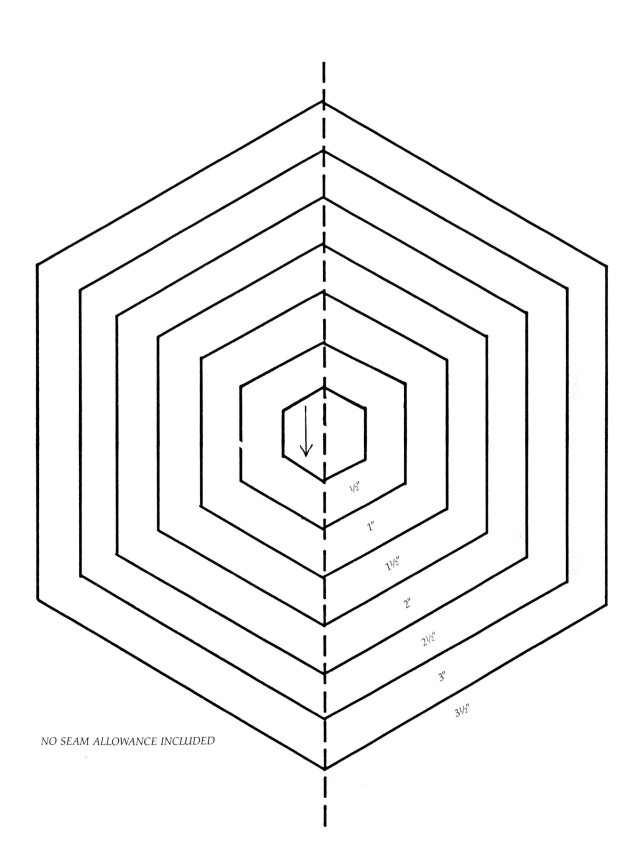

1/2"

1"

1 1/2"

2"

2 1/2"

3"

3 1/2"

NO SEAM ALLOWANCE INCLUDED

Translations

This chapter evolves out of the previous chapter in much the same way I suspect our traditional quilt patterns have evolved. One person started out with a simple design like *Shoo-Fly* and through one change or another a wonderful design, *Goose-In-The-Pond*, has emerged.

These changing designs make me think of the game of "Gossip," which we used to play. A group sits in a circle and one person begins by whispering a message to the person on his right. The message is whispered once and then passed on to the next person, then the next and the next. When the person at the end of the circle receives the message, he repeats it out loud to the group. Very rarely does the message come out intact. In fact, it's hard to figure how the message can change so much.

I didn't start out trying to translate quilt patterns. I have an irritating habit of reversing drawings, pictures and ideas. I may see something one way and draw it another. I may change it around without even realizing it until I have sewn the parts together. The habit annoyed me until I realized it gave me a little bit of creativity. I have a harder time when I am consciously trying to reverse pattern pieces.

The more I work with designs, the more I find my preferences falling into a pattern. Those I love are the tesselated designs that interlock and interweave. That is why I find I keep returning to the hexagon trying to find new uses for it among some of my old favorite patterns.

Most of the translations I have made are very simple. I have never felt the need to get too elaborate. Generally, I let the fabrics do that for me. You may think that some of my quilts look complicated, but basically I have used triangles, my curved hexagon, the log cabin and diamonds. I first decide on what design I want to use, then I design the whole quilt which is generally rather large and of a repetitive hexagon design. It is the fabric and the coloration that take the hours of decision-making. While I work on the quilt, I plan how the border should look. The border design is almost always based on some shape or part taken from the design of the inner quilt.

I could draw out many quilt designs for you, but I feel that half of the fun in quiltmaking is in the designing. What I want to do is show you how I would redraft some of the basic familiar patterns to use as hexagons. As long as I have been doing these translations, I have never really come up with a mathematical solution for the "how-to." It's a matter of looking at a design, analyzing it and then redrafting. Most of these presented here were done on the grid system shown in the previous chapters.

FOUR-PATCH DESIGNS

Bowtie
Divide two

Bowtie is a four-patch design which is broken down into four blocks: one large square plus small squares and triangles that repeat in reverse order on the second row.

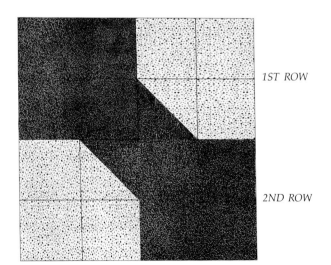

1ST ROW

2ND ROW

What makes *Bowtie* work in a translation is the repeat. The first row has two blocks, the large square and then the small squares and triangles. A hexagon is divided into six triangles.

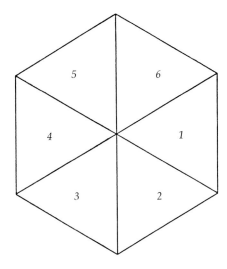

Make a hexagon grid divided by two. When you translate, the squares will become triangles. In the 1st row of *Bowties* you have one large square; this will become one large triangle (Triangle 1). Color in the first triangle in your hexagon. In Triangle 2 color in only the triangle nearest the center. Repeat two times to complete the entire hexagon (Triangle 3 and 4 and Triangle 5 and 6).

DIVIDE 2

2½"

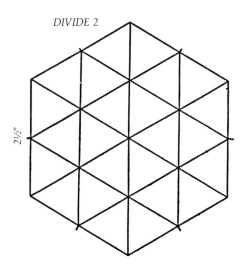

REPEAT

TRIANGLE 1

REPEAT

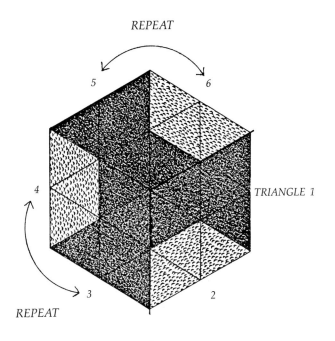

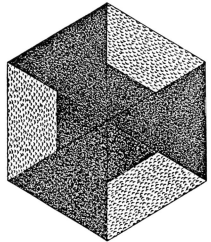

Ocean Waves
Divide four

This is a very elaborate four-patch (64 squares). One of the nice features is that it is already broken down into triangles—four across the bottom on the design.

 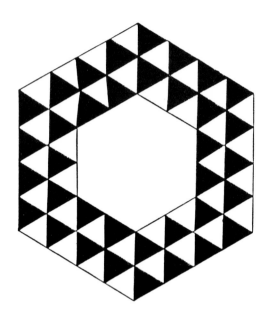

For this design you will have two templates, a hexagon and a triangle. My *Ocean Odyssey* quilt is a variation of the above design. To draft it I divided by three (you will have only one row of five triangles). Instead of a plain hexagon in the center, I used the curved hexagon.

Most of the four-patch designs that I came across were far too elaborate to translate. A lot could be done, but I came out with some nondescript designs so I decided to move on to eight-pointed stars. These proved to be a great resource and I want to share a few with you. The eight-pointed stars are also a repetitive design, one diamond repeated eight times. Translated into the hexagon, the star will be one diamond repeated only six times, but the look will be similar.

Stars

Evening Star
Divide two

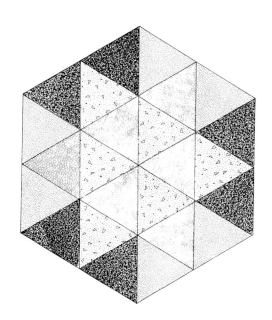

Blazing Star
Divide two

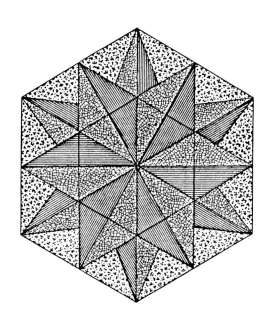

V Block
Divide two

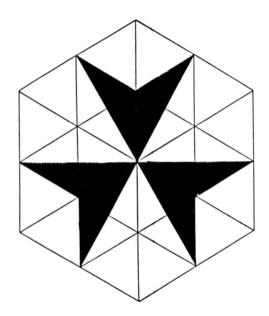

Dutch Rose
Divide four

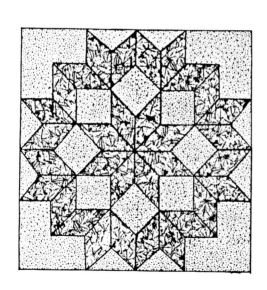

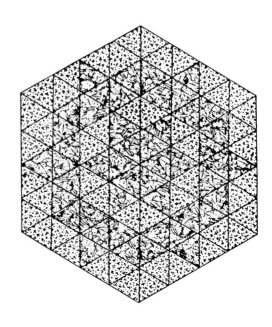

Flying Swallows
Divide four

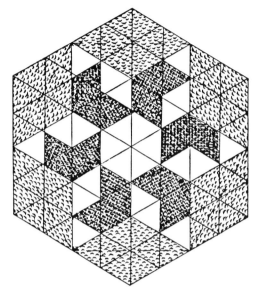

The background for this hexagon can be a triangle or a diamond. For triangle, make template along the broken line.

Forbidden Fruit Tree
Divide four

This is also a variation of the eight-pointed star. In the hexagon, you will have four triangle sections for the tree leaves and two sections for the tree trunk.

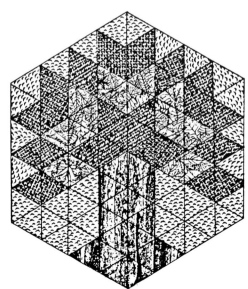

NINE-PATCH

Nine-patch designs seem to work out pretty well in translations. The nine-patch has three rows with three blocks in each row: a center surrounded by eight blocks. Translated, this could be *Grandmother's Flower Garden*: a center surrounded by six hexagons. Again, look for blocks that are simple and repeat patterns by two such as the following:

Shoo-Fly
Divide three

When breaking down the *Shoo-Fly* design for translation, start with the center—one block. On your hexagon grid find the center six triangles (this is your center hexagon). Color in. Surrounding the center block on the *Shoo-Fly* are repeating blocks of triangles and squares. Do the same thing on your hexagon grid. Color in one trapezoid (triangle block on *Shoo-Fly*) and the next hexagon will be plain (plain block on *Shoo-Fly*). Repeat two more times. It doesn't look anything like a *Shoo-Fly*. Depending on the fabric used, it could be any number of imaginative things.

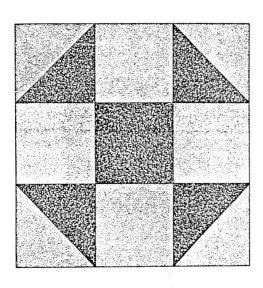
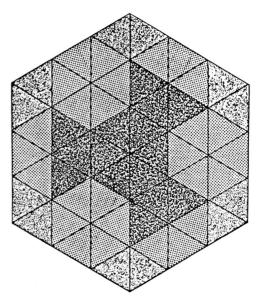

Air Castle
Divide three

 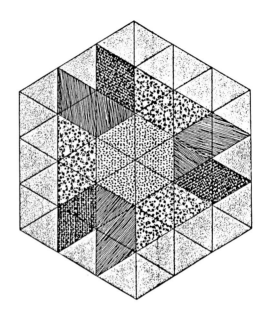

Ohio Star
Divide three

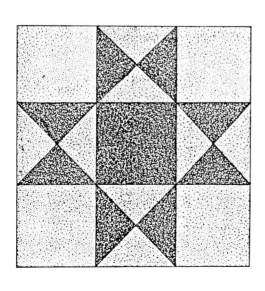 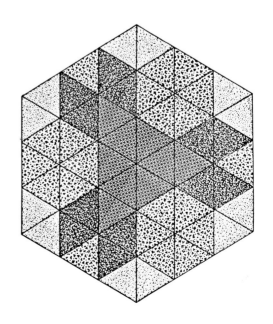

Baskets
Divide three

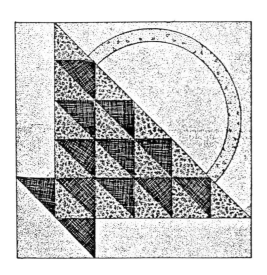

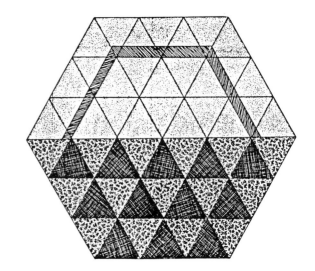

Finding designs with triangles as a base is helpful. This basket design fits perfectly into the hexagon shape. The pieced handle is drafted along the outer triangle row and measures one third of the triangle depth.

Pine Tree
Divide three

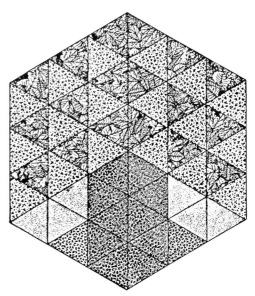

CURVES

Because I also love to work with curves, I had to include a few curve designs.

Drunkards Path
Divide two

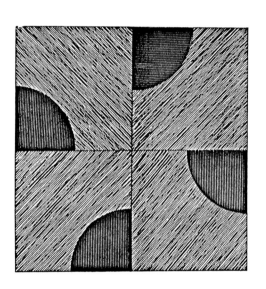

To get the curve, open compass to where the triangle is divided (this is half the compass opening), and draw your curve from left to right. With a ruler, place a notch mark in the center. (Remember the notches for all curved hexagons.) These are to ease fabric distribution.

Actually, you can make your compass opening any amount and create very small curves or large curves within the triangle. There is no rule.

Orange Peel

This is drawn with a compass. Open compass, any size, and draw hexagon. Do not change compass opening. Draw curves exactly the same as drawing the curved hexagon. After you draw this six times around the hexagon, reverse and draw curve six times going the other way. Close compass to half of compass opening, place point in center of design and mark notches on the curves.

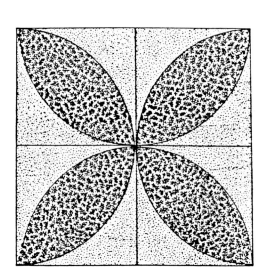
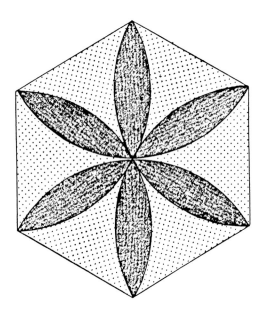

Robbing Peter to Pay Paul

This is the same design as *Orange Peel* except each petal is divided in half and the coloring is alternating light and dark. Mark notches.

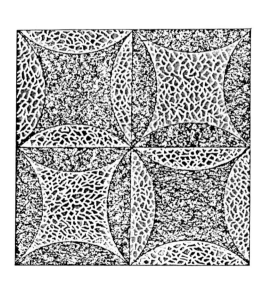

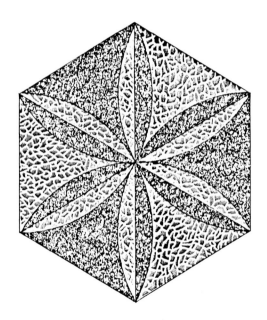

Log Cabin

This last example is a classic and extremely versatile design, one of my favorites.

Determine the finished size of your hexagon. Example: width 7″, length 8″, compass opening 4″ (refer to Hexagon Size Chart in Chapter II). Open compass to 4″ and draw a hexagon. Divide into six triangles. With a C-Thru ruler, start at outside and draw the first log ½″ wide. You will cross over your triangle line on the left and stop at the triangle line on your right. Rotate to the left and draw the next log. Keep moving to the left until you have six logs for the bottom row. Move up ½″ and draw your first log for Row C. Draw five more. Repeat instruction for Rows B and A until you have as many rows as you like. The center can be as big or small as you want it to be. The logs in each row will be of equal size.

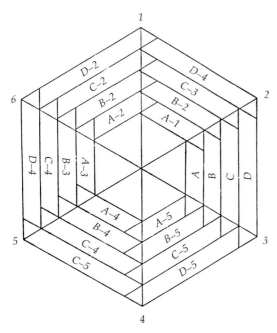

This pattern can now be used two ways: (1) With triangles separating the logs or (2) as a regular hexagon log cabin design with your triangle guide lines erased. In either case, transfer notch marks as I have them in the drawing.

To piece: If you are using the design with the logs and the triangles, piece the two together and then treat each piece as you would the regular log cabin. For both, stitch piece A to hexagon starting at notch, leaving left side free. Pin A-1 onto A and hexagon, stitch. Repeat with A-2, A-3, A-4 and A-5. Now pin A from notch to cover A-5 and sew. Repeat for Rows B, C and D.

If you make your log cabin hexagon a larger size, you might want to make the logs ¾″.

Shading Suggestions for Hexagon Log Cabin

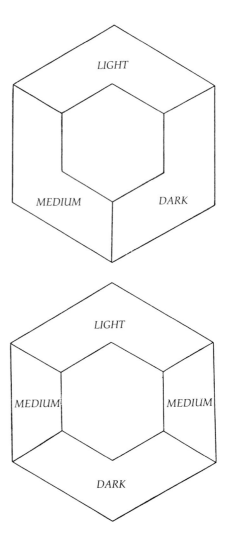

The Hexagon Sampler Quilt

If, after studying all these designs, you have trouble deciding which you would like to use in a quilt, why not make a hexagon sampler? Use the layout for the *Stone Wall* quilt with a 6½″ compass opening to draw all of your sampler patterns. Then refer to the lattice and diamond templates and border instructions for the *Stone Wall* quilt (Chapter V). The only change I would suggest is to use a half hexagon border instead of the curved border. This could include a variety of the fabrics that you use in all of the blocks. The corner block template will be drawn on the solid and the broken lines (see below).

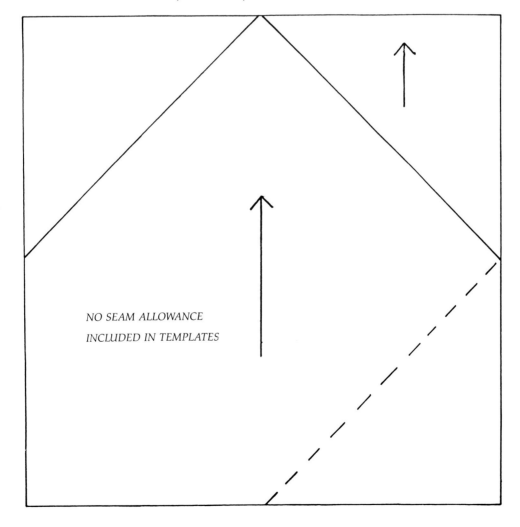

*NO SEAM ALLOWANCE
INCLUDED IN TEMPLATES*

The Quilt Setting

Once the basic design unit is chosen, the next major step is to select the proper setting. Because each setting is distinct and the proper setting plays a major role, I have some exercises that will help you decide. As you work through these exercises, one of the settings will reach out to you. It will "talk" to you, and you will reach an understanding with it. Making a quilt is like falling in love. Each step of the way can be idyllic, but there will be times, we all know, when you'll wonder how you got into this predicament. If you are in love with your project, you can overcome all obstacles.

With each step, you must be absolutely sure that you are creating *your* quilt. I can't stress this enough. If there is any hestitation, *stop*. Re-think what you are doing. Are you getting too much outside interference? Advice is fine, but instinct is better. Sometimes well-meaning friends and/or teachers will influence you into making *their* quilt. Think a lot about the choices you have made, and when you are positive you have figured out how you want your quilt to look, charge ahead. Most of all, be proud of what you are doing.

Playing around with the following exercises will give you a good feel for how the overall design will work in fabric. I have a theory: if you get bored working out your design in these preliminary stages then you can forget it in the fabric stage.

Throughout the following examples, I use a design that I "found"—one of the eight-pointed star examples. I call it *Birds;* you can rename it when you use it. It's okay to use any other hexagon design that you may like better, but to get familiar with the different settings use the same unit throughout these exercises. You begin by drafting *Birds* (compass opening 4") onto an 8½" x 11" piece of paper. Then rush to your local photocopy shop and have them reduce the design to a more manageable size,

say, about 1½" across. Make 100 copies. You don't want to be in the middle of one of the exercises and run out.

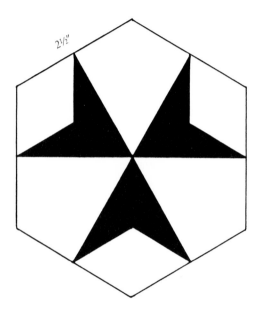

For the next few days pretend you are back in kindergarten. Freeing yourself up to play is a necessary and useful part of the creative process. I often find when I am working out one idea, I come up with another. Playing now is also a lot easier than making actual patches and then ripping out.

Cut out all of the 100 hexagons using paper scissors. You are now ready for a large glue stick. Using a separate sheet of paper for each setting, glue-stick your hexagons into each of the seven given here.

Mosaic

When the hexagons are grouped together in a mosaic setting a secondary design appears. it may or may not become more important than the original idea.

When glue-sticking your hexagons, be neat, but don't worry about perfection. Make enough rows so you can get a good idea of the overall design.

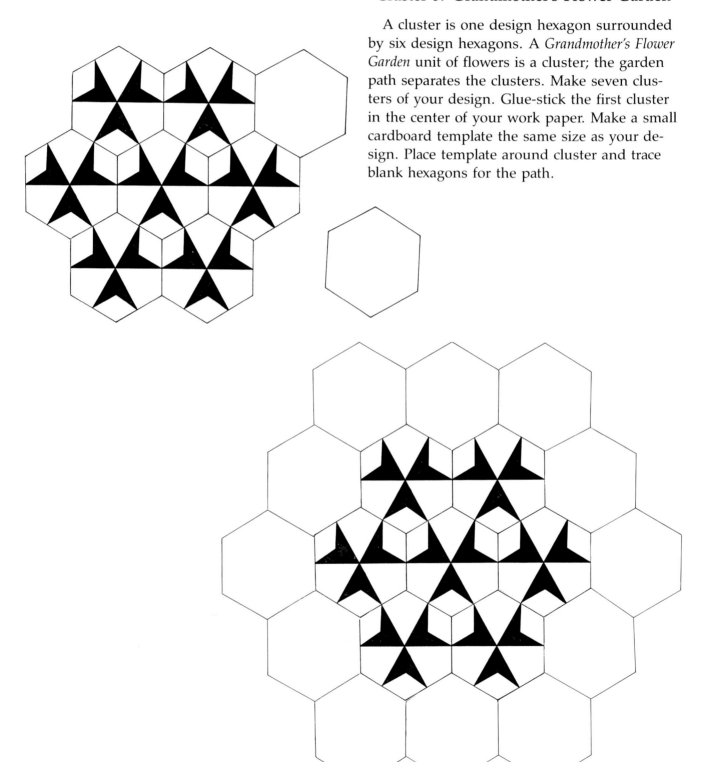

Cluster *or* Grandmother's Flower Garden

A cluster is one design hexagon surrounded by six design hexagons. A *Grandmother's Flower Garden* unit of flowers is a cluster; the garden path separates the clusters. Make seven clusters of your design. Glue-stick the first cluster in the center of your work paper. Make a small cardboard template the same size as your design. Place template around cluster and trace blank hexagons for the path.

Add surrounding clusters and draw additional blank paths.

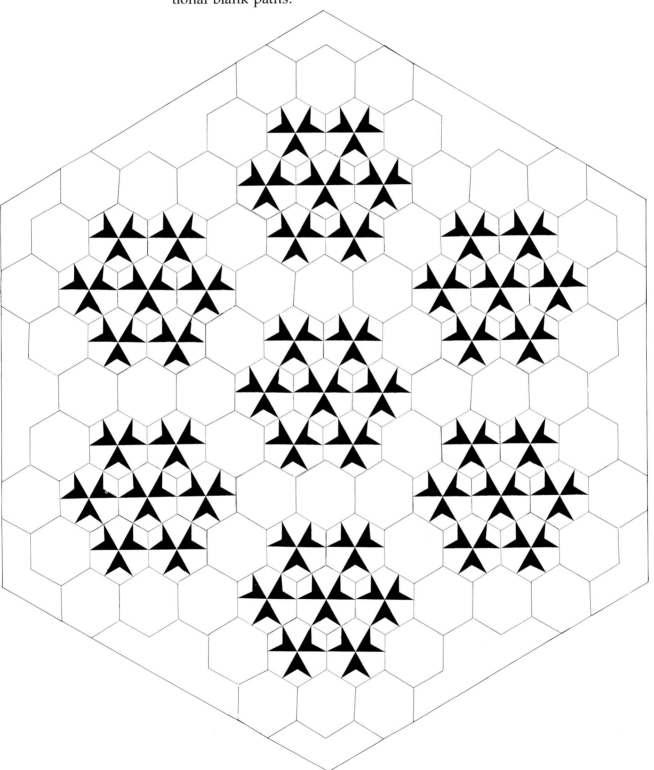

Baby Blocks

This might be interesting to try as a pyramid wall hanging. Glue-stick three hexagons for the bottom row. Add two and then one for top.

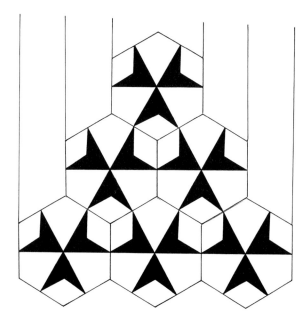

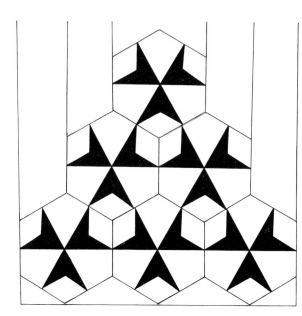

To square off this design, use a C-Thru ruler and draw lines with the sides of the hexagon as a guide.

For bottom line, place the ruler across tips of hexagons and draw a straight line.

For top line, measure from Row 1 hexagon tip (A) to Row 3 hexagon tip (B). This will give you the length. At right hand corner, mark up the dimension. Repeat at left corner. Draw line across top.

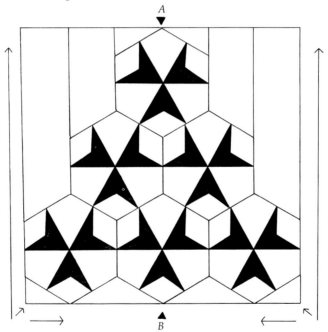

Lattice strips could be added to give a new design a traditional look.

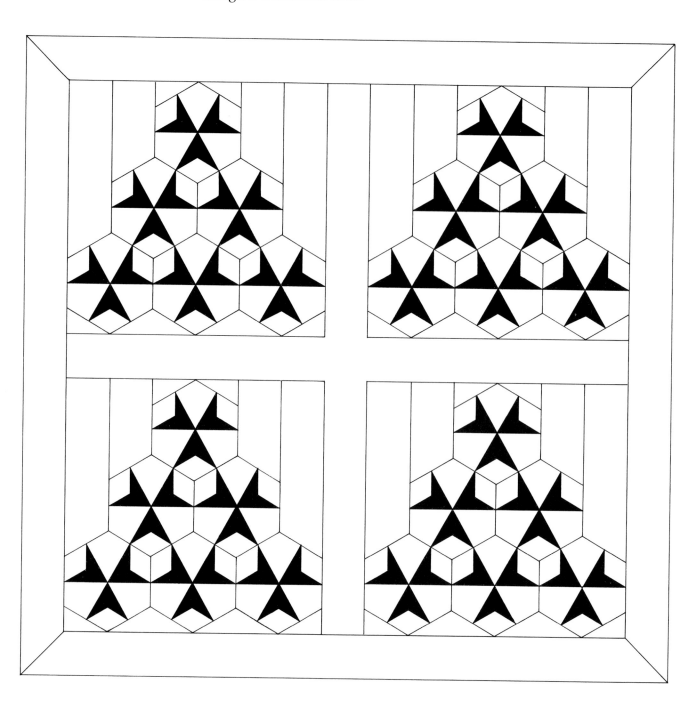

The dimensions for the lattice work will be determined by the size of the design finished block. The width of the background pieced section of the hexagon block would work well for the lattice strips and you could double the width for the borders.

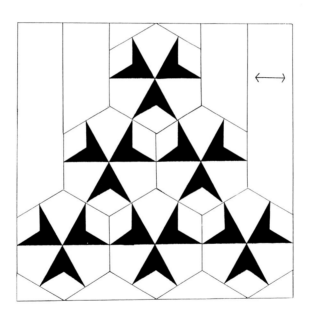

Hexagon Lattice No. 1

This is a *Grandmother's Flower Garden* setting with the addition of narrow lattice strips. When the hexagons are assembled, each design becomes distinct. The double strips of lattice make a strong statement.

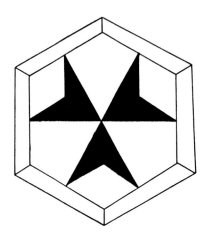

To draw the lattice, extend the triangle lines.

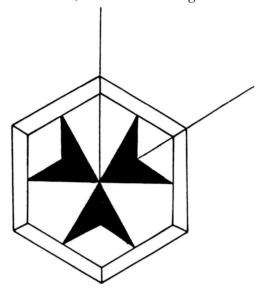

I like to use approximately one-eighth of the measurement of the triangle for the width of the strip. This is an arbitrary figure; it could be larger or smaller. You get a better sense of size when you draw your actual template.

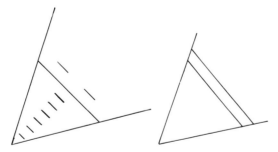

Make seven designs to glue-stick for overall pattern.

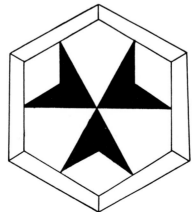

Hexagon Lattice No. 2

If you like the lattice setting idea, but would like a softer look and complement your design with intricate quilting, a single unit can be used in place of the double lattice. Use the same measuring method as in Lattice No. 1. Erase center line where lattice strips meet.

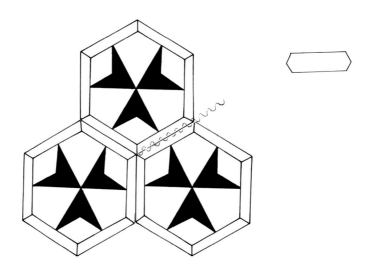

Block Style

Rows of hexagon units are separated by diamonds, making another area suitable for fancy
quilting. Glue-stick several rows of hexagons.
The diamond size will shape itself by the base
(compass opening) of the hexagons. Use your
30-60-90° triangle to draw a perfect diamond.

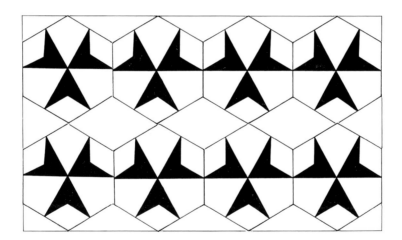

Hexagons and Triangles

This setting gives an illusion of hexagons floating. Size of the triangles will be base (compass opening) of the hexagons. Use 30-60-90° triangle to draw.

Hex-in-a-Hex

There are several ways to work this design:

1. Assemble three hexagon units. This will create a larger hexagon consisting of three design hexagons and three diamond background sections.

2. Assemble the three hexagons.

Cut a design hexagon into three diamonds and fill in the background.

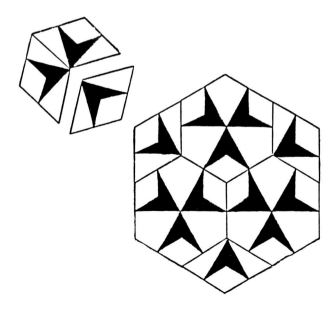

3. Turn the diamond design and fill in the background. This will slightly alter a design and can be used in a mosaic setting, lattice setting or any of the others shown here.

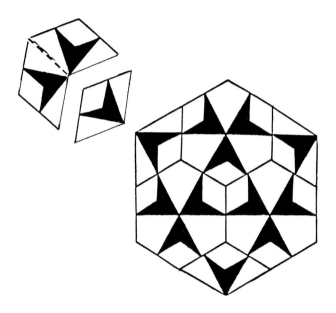

By now the *Birds* have put you off to a flying start. You have probably come up with a design idea or two of your own. Try them. The possibilities are endless.

Abstract Designs

Several years ago, in one of my hexagon workshops, a student had a wonderful idea for a design. She was working with a triangle and she wanted to incorporate a curve within the triangle. She played around until she came up with an interesting shape. It wasn't too difficult and she had several doodles on paper which she was thinking about using as a complete quilt. But, as we all know, most of us like to get right into fabrics and try just one part to see what it will look like. Well, she had quite a conglomeration of materials and as I looked at them I wasn't sure just what she was going to make out of it all. The scissors were flying and she was sewing away madly. When she started to put the piece together, her fabrics looked like a great hodgepodge and her curves didn't match up very well. I questioned her about this, and she said matter-of-factly that it was not important; she was more interested in the gentle curve of each piece and it was not necessary for the curves to match. Okay. I went about working with other students but kept wondering what was going to happen with this creation. Several times I went over to her and she was doing fine, she said, and how did I like her colors? I did think the colors were fine; but truly I did not fully understand what was happening here. When the class was nearing the end, I asked all the students for a show-and-tell so that we could see and hear how each person had carried out her idea. When the student with the quilt in question held it up, I was taken aback. It was truly beautiful and very exciting. Everyone was impressed. As she left the class, I said to those around me, "There goes a person with a magic mind and great vision."

Abstract quilts require a magic mind and great vision. People who work in abstracts have to have a complete understanding of their art, both technically and visually. Some ab-

stract work boggles my mind; I look at it and love it. Then again, there is other abstract art that makes me wonder if I'm being made the butt of a joke. It is very interesting. All of us interpret art in our own ways and sometimes we are on the same level as the artist and sometimes not. I am sure you have seen abstract quilts that strike your fancy. Once in awhile I am tempted to try an abstract quilt, but every time I have, I've not been comfortable with the creation of it. Some day perhaps.

Here are some ideas that may help you create an abstract quilt. Many people like to have a design to work with and then they will look for fabrics to interpret how they feel about that design. In creating these designs, I do not use the grid system because that makes the design look too traditional. Start by drawing a triangle.

It is not necessary to measure parts of the triangle into halves, quarters, etc. Just section off areas arbitrarily and shade in with a pencil.

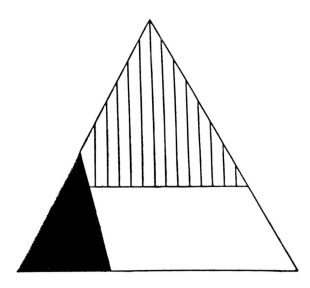

Once you have one triangle, try the following ways to set them together into a hexagon.

Six Triangles – Repeat

Butterfly

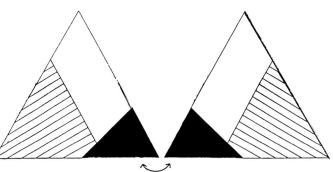

FLIP FLOP

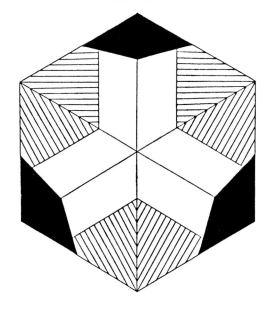

Triad

ROTATE

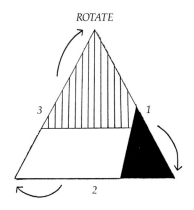

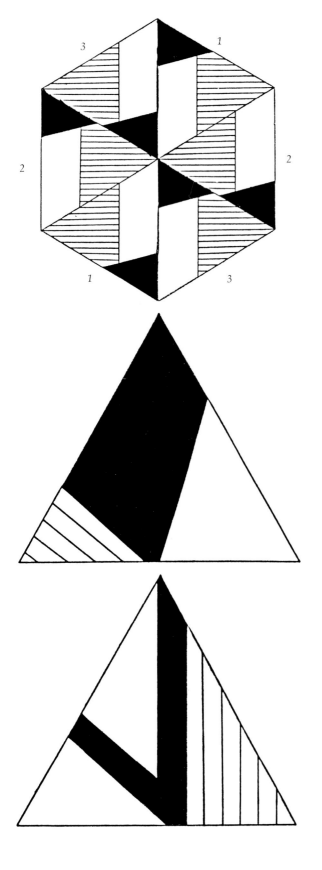

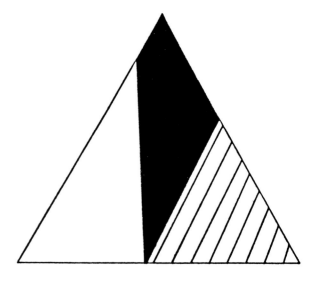

The idea can be very simple, leaving the major role to the fabric. If you tried this first design in the Repeat arrangement and used basically red fabrics, you could name it The Big Apple. Make your imagination work for you.

Your quilt could be a fantasy, the true meaning of which only you would know. In order to let the viewers explore their own imaginations, try giving your quilt a number instead of a name, say, Quilt No. 387. Or name your quilt by its colors—The Blue Quilt. That way people can interpret for themselves.

Children take to abstract much more readily than adults. They do not have a lot of preconceived notions of what it "should be" or "has to look like." They have wonderful imaginations. They can look at a picture or sculpture and envision what they would like it to be. Some very special adults have kept their imaginations flowing while studying design, color and construction. These are the true artists who create visually breathtaking pieces of abstract art whether it be in quilts, oils, watercolors, sculpture, ceramics or other mediums.

Here are a few more examples in abstract for you to explore:

Now make a photocopy of this triangle and hexagon and experiment with some ideas of your own:

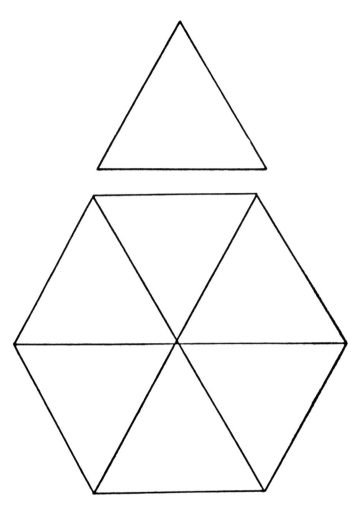

glass inside that created beautiful and exciting designs as you turned it. Rather it was a three-sided mirrored tube covered on the outside with velvet and open at both ends. When you held this about ¼″ above a line drawing and peered inside, it would give you a hexagon image of whatever you were looking at. This was a very easy way to find new ideas and to see right away if you might like a pattern as a hexagon.

If you can't find one to buy, you could try making it. At a glass and mirror shop, have three pieces of mirror cut 1½″ x 7″. Stand them upright in the shape of a triangular tube. Hold in place with a couple of elastic bands. Tape all around the three sides with black electrical tape. This will be a 3-way mirror when you are finished. You can cover over the electrician's tape with fabric to make it look pretty.

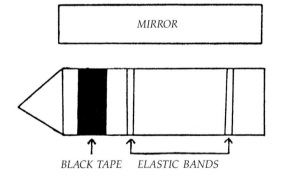

Once you have a design unit you think you might like to work into a quilt design, try using the ideas in some of the quilt settings in Chapter VII. When you work with an abstract idea, you can probably keep its abstract look by just setting the hexagons together as you would a mosaic. Once you start separating the hexagons with lattice or triangles you will give it a more traditional look. But experiment with the quilt settings. You never know what you may come up with.

Looking Through a Kaleidoscope

Several years ago, I bought a kaleidoscope in a quilt shop. It was not the kind with broken

Fabric Choices

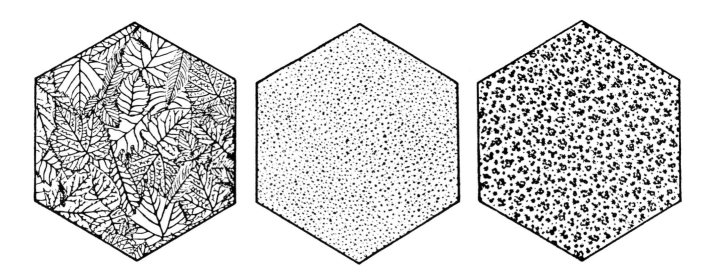

One of the major forces that draws quiltmakers to quilting is our love—our all-encompassing passion—for fabric. It's wonderful—wonderful to look at, to touch, to play with, to cut, to sew, to wear, to make drapes of and, best of all, to make quilts to snuggle under.

I can't remember a time in my life when I wasn't thinking of fabric. My mother made all of my clothes when I was small and I remember endless, boring hours of fittings and pinning of hems. The best part was shopping for fabrics. Mother had the neatest places for finding exciting materials. Of course, being in New England we had lots of mill stores (not so now). We bought yards off the bolt, or small pieces from bins. The choicest goodies were those sold by the pound.

My all-time favorite fabric was a Dan River red plaid cotton we found in one of those mill stores. I made it into a shirtwaist dress for my first-day-of-school outfit when I entered ninth grade. I put brass buttons down the front of that dress and it became my special dress for years and years. I loved the dress so much that

15 years later, when I finally decided it was time for a change, I re-made it into a pair of overalls for my firstborn. The fabric was still in excellent condition.

My mother still wanted me to make a couple of outfits a year when I was in high school, even though store-bought clothing seemed more appealing at the time. Fortunately, all my friends sewed and we delighted in the fact that we could run home from the store with a piece of fabric and whip up a skirt in one evening. This sewing experience was invaluable to me because I was tall, and the selection at the "Tall Girls" Shop was really limited. Also, my clothes were always different from other people's. To this day I find it much easier to sew my own than to go shopping, and I like my one-of-a-kind clothing.

Sewing clothes led me to drapery making. I was able to custom-make draperies and bedspreads as a business when my children were little. My first classes were in drapery making. And this led me into quilting.

I had not made my own quilt before I started my first class (though I was working with a group on a quilt). My students chose a quilt pattern and each made a quilt over the 20-week course. We worked out the technical details together and if a problem was beyond me, I would ask Gram or try to work it out during the week between classes. The course was successful. Everyone finished a beautiful quilt by the end of the year and not till then did someone think to ask me "how many" quilts I had made. I did confess.

By this time, I had chosen a pattern for my own quilt, The *Double Wedding Ring*. I wanted to make it with lots of scraps, but my fabrics were really not suitable. At that time, polyester clothing was popular and I knew I wanted to use cottons. The fabric shops didn't have much to offer so I started going to thrift shops and collecting all the old cotton blouses, skirts and aprons I could find. When the clerks found out about my project, they helped me enthusiastically. I ended up with tons of fabrics, some of which I am still using. Today thrift shops have lots of polyester and scarcely any cotton. I made my *Double Wedding Ring* and loved every minute of it. It actually marked the end of my drapery business, though not my penchant for drapery fabrics.

If you haven't already, you should take a trip to the drapery section of your fabric shop and look at all the wonderful cottons offered there. The colors are beautiful and the designs are rich. They may seem a little heavy if you have only used cotton calicoes, but once they are washed they soften up. I also scout around in the upholstery section. My New England thriftiness makes me want to add that these fabrics are usually quite wide, so you get a lot for your money.

Generally, I have an idea for a quilt before I even think of fabric, as in the *Ocean Odyssey* quilt I told about in Chapter V. Pieces of the 72 yards of material I had amassed for that one quilt have filtered into practically every quilt I

have made since. Some other special pieces have too. After the first New England Images Show, which was sponsored by the New England Quilters Guild, and for which I served as chairman, the committee gave me a fabric shower. The gifts were to be "purple" fabrics. They knew I used most any type of material, so they gave me cottons, blends, upholstery, drapery, linings, satin and some just plain "stuff." The Guild asked me to be their speaker at the April 1985 meeting and I decided secretly to make a quilt using this very special collection of material. The *Little Fishes* (cover photo) was the result. I used at least one piece of everyone's fabric in it proving to me that the more fabric you use and the greater the variety in texture, the more interesting the quilt becomes.

You can blend the beautiful and the ugly, the "musts" with the "impossible." Both *Ocean Odyssey* and *The Little Fishes* are basically purple quilts. But look at the range of colors in each, from the very palest of lavender to the deepest of purple. *Ocean Odyssey* also has a "zap" color of red and touches of green. Most of the fabrics that people have enjoyed seeing in *The Little Fishes* have been the unusual ones: the upholstery, the drapery, the lining. They balance the exquisite pieces of Hoffman prints and imported cotton from China.

Though upholstery, drapery and lining materials may not be the easiest to use, they are not that difficult. All the *Fishes* fabric was prewashed and dried in the dryer so that the quilt is usable. When people express concern about the life of unusual fabrics, I can only tell them about my experience. When I first started making quilts, I used mainly cotton/blends. These were very nice broadcloths and also some not so good cotton/poly blends. The quilts made with both have done very well. These are quilts I made for our family's use. They were heavily quilted and have had rough and tumble use. The children's friends sit on them, they get tossed on the floor, they get rolled up and used for sleeping bags, and the dog and cat sleep on them if they can't get under them. The only special treatment quilts get at our house is lots of love. The fabrics have not worn and the colors are still nice and bright. When I hear people downgrade the blends, I think of my own experiences and have nothing but good comments to offer.

Sure they may be a little (and I emphasize that word little) harder to work with and your quilting stitches may not be as even, but for durability and strength, I highly recommend blends. Just make sure to use your templates with *no seam* allowance, trace and cut your fab-

rics very carefully, and sew slowly on your guidelines.

Liking to use all kinds of materials in my quilts may be part of my New England heritage. Our great grandmothers used whatever they had available, and that is what I love about the old quilts. Today's stores are filled with all kinds of fabrics, from beautiful cotton calicoes, the dressmaker's blends, corduroy, wool, challis prints, silks, drapery and upholstery fabrics to heaven-knows what. With these choices you owe it to yourself to experiment. Mix something unusual with your cottons and your calicoes. Use the large prints with the small prints. The solids with the plaids. The silks and satins with cotton and corduroy. Try it, you might like it.

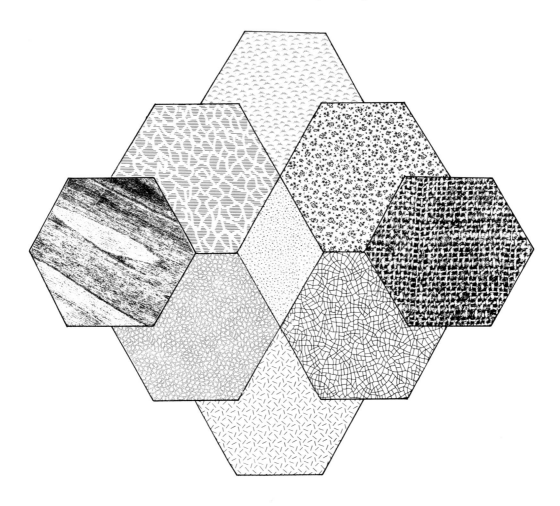

A novel experiment is to cut a large overall print into small pieces (I used 1½" triangles in *Paprika*) and to discover how many different colors and shapes you get from just one material. This works with any shape as long as you don't cut the pieces too big. You can get a whole new perspective with one wild and crazy print or subtle shading from a moiré fabric.

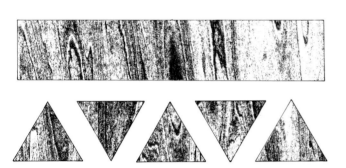

It is important for us to remember that fabric is terminal, and that a quilt does have a lifespan. Yes, I realize that we put hundreds of hours into our beloved quilts. But we also make quilts to be used (either on beds or to be exhibited) and eventually a day will come when one comes out of the washing machine in a terminal state. That is truly a very sad experience. But one has to think of the many wonderful years people have enjoyed sleeping under that quilt, cuddling into it when they were sick or feeling blue, not to mention the sheer pleasure of looking at it.

One says goodbye, and then comes the joy of starting a new quilt! When I made my first quilts, I made them for my children and dreamed about their passing them onto their children. I have since made the children each two more quilts (all still in pretty good shape), and I am sure that when they marry and have children, it will give me great pleasure to make lots of new quilts for each occasion.

If we make quilts to be preserved only in closets, we run the risk of damaging the pleasure of future generations of quiltmakers. Why should they make quilts when the market will be flooded with hundreds and hundreds of quilts that the antique dealers and collectors will find in our homes, unused and untouched? Why should we pass along fabulous collections of fabrics, which our children may never appreciate as much as we do? They will have no need to create; we will have taken that pleasure from them. We need to make quilts for ourselves and our children and all the people we love *now*. Most of us hardly need to be reminded that the pleasure received from making and giving a quilt cannot be described.

118

Finishing Techniques

Deciding on the borders, background or edges of a quilt is almost as difficult as working out the focal point. Many of my quilts have jagged edges: *Black Widow Spider*, *Reflection*, *Snowflakes*, *Poinsettia* and *Leaves In the River* . I thought that this was the best way to finish them because I had already made my statement and had nothing more to say. Quilts with odd edges are difficult to hang in quilt shows, alas. Unless they are against a blank wall, they get lost among the large quilts, and the backs of other people's larger quilts behind them usually do not coordinate. My solution to the problem was to make backgrounds from pieces of fabric several inches larger than the quilts themselves. (Make a narrow hem all around the fabric and sew a sleeve across the top.) Two of the backgrounds I made are of velvet. One I sewed onto the background fabric and another I pinned. I made a separate machine-quilted background for *Poinsettia* and sewed it and the quilt together. A background not only makes it easier to hang the quilt, but in a show it frames the quilt with the right backdrop.

Many hexagon quilts don't need additional borders, as I said. All that is required is background filler to square off your quilt. The *Clown* quilt is a good example of the clowns taking over the entire quilt; the background triangles are used only to square off the piece for hanging or for bed use. The choice of color will depend on where you are using the quilt. Black is an excellent filler for a wall hanging because it makes the quilt look matted. Light solid colors such as white, off-white and pale pastels tend to give a "floating" feeling.

The background for *The Little Fishes* had me puzzled for a while. After piecing all those triangles for the fishes, I just didn't have the heart to fill in with large pieces of plain or even printed fabrics. I wanted to continue with the water effect and the only way to achieve that was to piece hundreds of triangles in a variety of colors. What a job, but I loved the results.

Then I didn't know what to do with the edges. Somehow putting a border didn't seem right and just finishing it off with binding wasn't enough. That's when I decided *Dune Points* were called for. *Dune Points* are New England's answer to *Prairie Points*. We have dunes in New England, not prairies. *The Little Fishes* was the perfect quilt on which to try *Dune Points*. I used a lightweight splashy print drapery fabric and the results blend perfectly with the entire quilt. You need approximately 184 hexagons for an 80" x 90" quilt and 2¼ yards of 40" to 44" fabric.

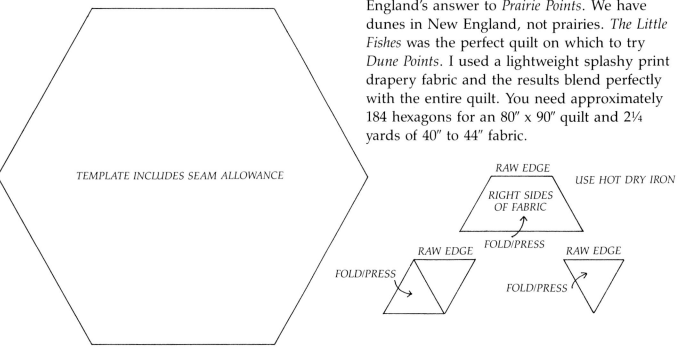

TEMPLATE INCLUDES SEAM ALLOWANCE

RAW EDGE

USE HOT DRY IRON

RIGHT SIDES OF FABRIC

FOLD/PRESS

RAW EDGE

RAW EDGE

FOLD/PRESS

FOLD/PRESS

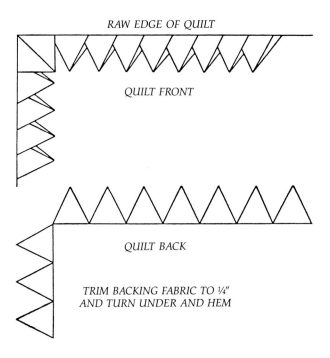

RAW EDGE OF QUILT

QUILT FRONT

QUILT BACK

TRIM BACKING FABRIC TO ¼"
AND TURN UNDER AND HEM

After my problems with exhibiting quilts with unusual edges, I decided I had better try finishing them as rectangles. Both *Ocean Odyssey* and *The Good Earth* needed straight edges and borders to complete the picture. In *Ocean Odyssey*, I used the curved hexagon and then strips to make up the outer edge, blending the fabrics from one row into the next. This drawing shows part of the border for *Ocean Odyssey*; I used a narrow border, then a patchwork border and finally an outer border. Notice how I blended the inner border with a section of the patchwork and the outer border with the second color of the patchwork.

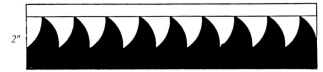

2"

In *Good Earth* I used that same idea working with a triangle. In the process of making a quilt, you will probably discover a shape you are working with that would make up well in the border.

When you aren't able to divide your borders evenly, you will have to make two different templates—one for the sides and another for the top and bottom. As long as you keep the width of the borders the same, you can change the length of the shape you are using.

When I made *Stone Wall*, it was a definite block style quilt and I felt a border was needed to finish it properly. It is when I am making the content of a quilt that I think about how to finish it, not beforehand. This is a process that I can only describe as living with what I am doing, getting acquainted with the work and then deciding how it should continue and end. When I start an idea I do have a "game plan," and I have a good feel for what I want it to look like. I also draw pictures, graphs and play with colored pencils trying to express what I'd like the quilt to look like. But somehow I always do spend a lot of time ripping apart and putting things back together again. Sometimes I wonder if it wouldn't be easier to throw the whole thing out and start again, but I don't. I persevere (often with a lot of encouragement from friends) and finally I reach my goal. The process is something that each individual has to work out alone. If you can put down on paper exactly what you want and follow through each step, I take my hat off to you.

A Triangle Border

2½"

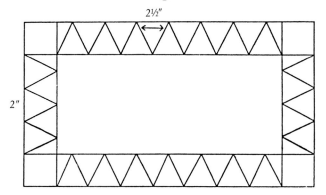

2"

Borders can make or break your quilt. Because patchwork stretches, use graph paper for making your measurements. Refer back to the *Stone Wall* quilt directions and the notch technique if you are applying patchwork borders. If you have made changes in your quilt as you have worked, make these changes on your graph paper too. Then when you make a decision on your background and borders, you can incorporate the changes on your graph paper and you will have the exact measurements to cut. The result will be nice straight even borders.

The *Boston Garden* quilt is basically a floating pieced *Grandmother's Flower Garden*. After the piece work was completed, I went back to my graph paper and drew in the outer diamonds and triangles. Then I could calculate the size of the outer border and draw the miters.

Border Strips

If you make a picture-frame kind of border, you want to guard against giving the appearance of putting a lot of work into the center section of your quilt and then getting tired of the whole project. Have the borders complement the interior, whether it be patchwork or plain stripes.

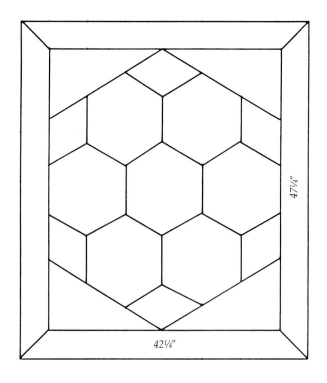

47¼"

42¼"

These measurements *include* ¼" seam allowance. Cut on lengthwise grain of fabric.

Measure and cut two strips 5" by 42¾"
Measure and cut two strips 5" by 47¾"

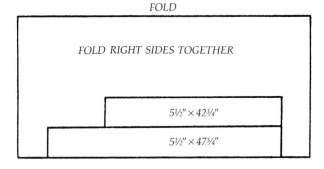

FOLD

FOLD RIGHT SIDES TOGETHER

5½" × 42¾"

5½" × 47¾"

Mark the ¼" seam allowance all around the edges on all border strips. On each strip, measure in 5" from the ¼" seam allowance and mark a notch. Do this at either end of each border strip (this is the allowance for mitering). Divide the remainder of the strip into quarters. Divide the pieced top into quarters on each side. Mark notches at these intersections.

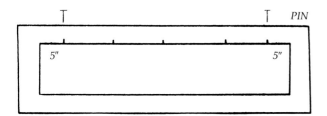

Pin 47¾″ border to side of quilt starting at 5″ notch. Match notches all along side of quilt, easing fabric if necessary and ending with 5″. Stitch, starting at pin and ending with pin, along pencil guide lines. Pin the other side and stitch.

Divide the quilt into quarters along the top and bottom. Pin and stitch the 42¾″ strips to top and bottom of quilt. You will have 5″ (plus seam allowance) left at either end of all the strips.

To miter corners fold quilt in half on the diagonal. Line up the lengths of the borders. Draw a line across the unstitched portion of the border, starting from the end of stitching to the outer edge of the fabric. Don't try to stitch this without marking. You will be stitching across the grain and the fabric will probably stretch. Pin along drawn line. Stitch from inside to outside edge. After checking the front of the quilt for accuracy, cut away excess material. Repeat to miter the three additional corners.

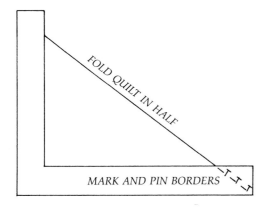

I hope I have given you enough hints with borders. Because each design is different and every person's interpretation is unique, the quilt you work on will be totally yours. Enjoy this process. At times it can be totally frustrating but there are times it can be like rolling off a log.

Again, I have to admit that every quilt I make gets taken apart at least three times. I hate ripping. I also hate to waste fabric, but sometimes the material you thought would be perfect just does not work. Keep on looking. You can always save the other material for another project, or swap with someone else.

It seems that I have to look at a design in fabric before I can finally decide whether it will be a yes or no. When you have made the right decision, you will know. Your quilt will sing.

Quilting

Deciding on a quilting design, again, is a very personal thing. Many people like to quilt ¼″ in around each patch. Some people like quilting in the ditch and some like elaborate feather or other designs. I like lots of different styles and, again, I make my decision while working on my quilt. Many times I quilt the hexagons (or the design hexagon) in the ditch and then go back and quilt a design over the patchwork area. I like to use the tear drop inside triangles. To draw, use a compass for the circle and draw the curves freehand.

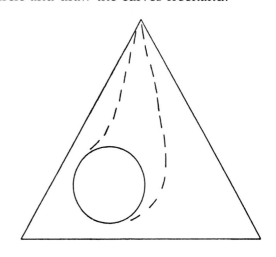

Sometimes I doodle:

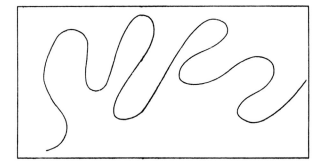

When I doodle, I quilt all the patched hexagons in the ditch and then go back and mark the quilt freehand. Try this on a piece of paper; I bet you did this in school when the teacher got boring and you just didn't know what to do with yourself. If you are using a plain color backing on your quilt, it's easier to mark and sew on the back. Just relax and do it. It gives the quilt a free moving feeling, and I like to quilt in this manner to highlight details like water, rain and wind.

Some quilts seem to demand lots of straight neat lines. Mark them with a ruler and pencil, or try masking tape.

Quilting gives another dimension both to the quilt and the quilter. Quilting is very soothing. I spend at least two hours every day quilting. Many times I will work four or five hours (with breaks) if I have a deadline to meet or just want to take a day off from other activities. If I do not have a design of my own to quilt, I will quilt an antique top.

There are times when you may want to do something quick and easy. That's when you should try machine-quilting a top. Machine-quilted quilts are very durable, especially for children. Even though most of my quilts are hand quilted, I do them either way. *Clowning Around* is all machine quilted. Quilting a large quilt on the machine is not so hard if you baste all your layers together in reverse. Layer the quilt with the pieced top on the bottom, next the batting, then the quilt back on top. Baste. Now the big loops will be on the back side and the front of the quilt will have tiny basting stitches. This avoids having your thread get caught up in the machine foot. On large quilts, I stick to pretty straight lines. But when you feel confident, you certainly can do fancy work as well. It is important to remember, you want your quilt to look just as nice and neat as if you were quilting in a frame or hoop. So keep checking the back and do not let it pucker.

Binding

I always have mixed emotions about coming to the end of a quilt. I'm happy that it's almost finished, excited that my vision is about to become a reality, and sad because the quilt has consumed so much of me and my time and I don't want to stop. It's like facing the final pages of a great book. I've made a wonderful attachment and am reluctant to let go. One of the things that takes the edge off the sadness is putting my mind on the binding.

When cutting the strips of cloth for the binding, you can use the crosswise grain of the fabric or cut on the bias. Generally, I use the crosswise grain because I am using fabric left over from the quilt, and I never seem to have a piece big enough to cut on the bias.

Cut strips of cloth 2½" wide by the width of your fabric (44" to 45"). Stitch pieces together to make a length to go around your quilt. Measure all four sides of your quilt and add 10". Fold binding in half lengthwise (wrong sides together) forming a double binding with one edge raw and the other finished. Fold end in about 1". Pin binding to front of quilt, raw edges together, along one side. Machine stitch through all thicknesses using a very loose stitch (about six stitches to the inch). Stop stitching ¼″ from end of row. Backstitch. Remove quilt from machine and measure ½″ of binding. Make a pleat by folding the ½″ of fabric in half. This excess fabric will form the binding mitered corner. Do not stitch. Pleat will be above raw edge of quilt. See diagram. Pin pleat in place ¼″ down from top raw edge and start pinning binding all along raw edge of the side of quilt until you reach ¼″ from the bottom. Stitch binding, leaving ¼″ seam allowance at either end. Backstitch when you start and stop stitching. Remove quilt from machine and make a pleat each time you come to a corner. A square quilt will have four corners and a quilt with jagged edges will have many corners. To finish, lap approximately 2″ of binding over folded end at beginning of binding.

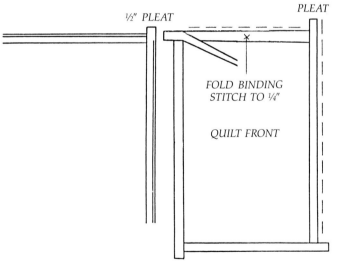

½″ PLEAT *PLEAT*

FOLD BINDING STITCH TO ¼″

QUILT FRONT

Remove quilt from machine and check back to see if fabric is smooth. Cut away excess fabric and batting leaving ¼″ seam allowance of binding, quilt batting and backing. Fold binding over seam allowance and hand stitch along stitched line. Miter corner where fabric pleat is. Binding will show on front and back. Embroider your name and date on back of quilt.

HAND STITCH BINDING ALONG SEAM LINE TUCK IN PLEAT FABRIC IN BACK TO FORM MITER ON BOTH SIDES

Now that the quilt is finished, it is time to show it off. Your family and friends will love it and they will say all kinds of flattering things about the quilt and your talent. It is a good feeling to make quilts for people you love and when you finish doing that you can make quilts for yourself and to exhibit in shows. There is something special about having your quilts in a show, in sharing your work.

I trust that I have opened the doors to hexagons for you and given you the courage to try experimenting with this clever design. I have shared my love of quilting with you and hope after you have completed a project you will share yours with me. As I said more than once, I find that the more I work with hexagons, the more I discover. Perhaps this will happen to you. Take time to work at it, especially the pattern drafting. Learning to draft will give you the power and freedom to create.

Please feel free to challenge anything I have written in this book. I have taught myself most of these techniques and so far they have worked well, but I am always finding new ways of doing my work and am constantly changing. So if you find a method or technique different from mine and it works well for you, do it. As we all know, the joy is in the doing—as well as in the sharing.

BIBLIOGRAPHY

126

Beyer, Jinny, *Patchwork Patterns*, Virginia; EPM Publications, Inc., 1979

Elwin, Janet B., *Ode to Grandmother*, Mass.; self published, 1986

Gutcheon, Jeffrey, *Diamond Patchwork*, New York; Alchemy Press, 1982

Hall, Carrie A. and Kretsinger, Rose G., *The Romance of the Patchwork Quilts*, New York, Bonanza Books, no date. © 1935 by Caxton Printers, Inc., Caldwell, Idaho Ickis, Marguerite, *The Standard Book of Quilt Making and Collecting*, New York; Dover Publications, 1949

McKim, Ruby Short, New York; Dover Publications, 1962

Mills, Susan Winter, New York; Arco Publishing, Inc., 1980

Sneum, Gunnar, *Teaching Design & Form*; Reinhold Publishing Corp., 1965

ACKNOWLEDGMENTS

Quiltmaking, for me, is very solitary work. Without the people at my classes, workshops and lectures who always renew my energy and excitement I could not have spent the hundreds of hours it takes to create each quilt I make. Writing this book has been a similar experience. I am indebted not only to my eager, willing students who went along with my many experimental projects but also to the sewing lessons from my Mother, the quilting parties with Gram, the opportunity to work at home while Mark, Toby and Lea were growing up, and to Bill and Dave for always being there. My work reflects my life and all those who have been a part of it.